Routledge I

Modern Child

First published in 1948, *Modern Child*
marised account of the most important wo
1940s. A vast amount of careful research o
development has been undertaken and m
Bowley has attempted to outline in
important findings of the psychoanalytic
analysis have had far reaching and revolu
bringing up children. Probably the con
have done more to change the outlook o
school of thought.

This important historical reference wor
developmental psychology, child psycholo

Modern Child Psychology

Agatha H. Bowley

First published in 1948
by Hutchinson's University Library.

This edition first published in 2025 by Routledge
4 Park Square, Milton Park, Abingdon, Oxon, OX14 4RN

and by Routledge
605 Third Avenue, New York, NY 10017

Routledge is an imprint of the Taylor & Francis Group, an informa business

© 1948 Agatha H. Bowley

All rights reserved. No part of this book may be reprinted or reproduced or utilised in any form or by any electronic, mechanical, or other means, now known or hereafter invented, including photocopying and recording, or in any information storage or retrieval system, without permission in writing from the publishers.

Publisher's Note
The publisher has gone to great lengths to ensure the quality of this reprint but points out that some imperfections in the original copies may be apparent.

Disclaimer
The publisher has made every effort to trace copyright holders and welcomes correspondence from those they have been unable to contact.

A Library of Congress record exists under ISBN: 50013221

ISBN: 978-1-041-02758-4 (hbk)
ISBN: 978-1-003-62087-7 (ebk)
ISBN: 978-1-041-02761-4 (pbk)

Book DOI 10.4324/9781003620877

MODERN
CHILD PSYCHOLOGY

by

AGATHA H. BOWLEY, B.A., PH.D.,
SENIOR PSYCHOLOGIST, LEICESTER SCHOOL
PSYCHOLOGICAL SERVICE.

HUTCHINSON'S UNIVERSITY LIBRARY
11 Stratford Place, London, W.1
New York   Melbourne   Sydney   Cape Town

THIS VOLUME IS NUMBER 20 IN
HUTCHINSON'S UNIVERSITY LIBRARY

CONTENTS *Page*

Introduction 7

Section I

RESEARCH WORK IN CHILD PSYCHOLOGY

Chapter	I	The Biographical Method	13
	II	The Observational Method	15
	III	The Experimental Method	29
	IV	The Interview Method	34
	V	The Psychometric Method	39
	VI	The Questionnaire Method	44
		References	47

Section II

RESULTS. FACTS CONCERNING THE
NORMAL DEVELOPMENT OF THE CHILD

Chapter	I	Babyhood	51
	II	The Child in the Nursery	63
	III	The Child in the School	82
	IV	The Young Person in Society	96
		References	106

Section III

CHARTS OF NORMAL DEVELOPMENT

Section IV

PSYCHO-ANALYTIC THEORY AND METHOD IN RELATION
TO DEVELOPMENT DURING THE FIRST TWO YEARS

References 128

Section V

SOME APPLICATIONS OF CHILD PSYCHOLOGY

Chapter	I	A School Psychological Service—The School and the Child	133
	II	The War and the Child	143
		References	151

INTRODUCTION

I N these days of cataclysmic wars, of atomic energy, of radar, of television and rapidity of transport, man has found himself to be master of the physical universe in a sense hitherto undreamed. Yet human nature remains remarkably frail and fallible. As Emmanuel Miller has remarked, "man has still the mind of a child and is yet handling the instruments of an adult." Although we set up vast international organizations to control the actions of nations, man himself remains at the mercy of his inner emotions and instincts to a large extent. At heart he is a savage; at times he burns with aggression, hate, jealousy and envy. Although his primitive feelings are controlled in some measure by external restrictions—by parents, by the Church, and by the State, and in some measure by his own conscience and personal ethics, he is liable to outbreaks of crime or war or unreliable conduct.

Modern psychology has made exhaustive studies of man. We have discovered that the root of the trouble lies in childhood; that early relationships and the problems of early development are all-important. There has been a minor revolution in our attitude towards children. We no longer regard the infant as the adult in miniature. The fact that we no longer dress him in miniature adult clothes is an indication of our changed attitude. We expect him to be noisy and untidy and rebellious and non-co-operative and lively at times—in fact we expect him to be childish. Growing-up we recognize to be a tedious and often painful business and difficulties are liable to occur on the way.

We no longer expect young children to work in mines and factories. We demand free education, free milk, free meals, free medical advice, reasonable housing and family allowances. Most of these are now considered to be the child's birthright. Moreover, very special provision is made for the handicapped and maladjusted child. The child is beginning to come into

8 MODERN CHILD PSYCHOLOGY

his own. Given adequate home standards and good provision for growth and development, given outlet for emotions and instincts in his childhood play, we are less likely to have to face so many problems of human misunderstanding and friction in adulthood.

Moreover our ideas about discipline and child care have radically altered. We have, I think, now passed through the stage of believing in free discipline, which meant a kind of Liberty Hall to all, and was, no doubt, a reaction to Victorian methods. We now recognize the value to a child of a stabilized background, wise standards and intelligent discipline based on true affection for the child. The father of the family is no longer a patriarch of the Mr. Barrett of Wimpole Street pattern. He tends to be a much more understanding and human individual who knows how to love as well as to discipline his children.

In this book I intend to give a summarized account of the most important work on child psychology. A vast amount of careful research on the problems and the progress of development has been undertaken and much valuable data obtained. We are no longer working altogether in the dark. Psychological studies and findings have had a tremendous effect on education and the companion volume on educational psychology will give a full account of this development. We can also now pride ourselves on the fact that we know something about the inner levels of the mind as well as the outer. We know not only when a child is likely to talk, but also something about the way he is likely to think and feel. This is, of course, extremely important, and though in this sphere we may often have to deal with hypotheses rather than facts, evidence is accumulating of the immense influence of the unconscious mind on conscious actions and behaviour.

I have also attempted to outline in non-technical language the most important findings of the psycho-analytic school. The discoveries of psycho-analysis have had far-reaching and revolutionary effects on our methods of bringing up children. Probably the contributions of Freudian psychology have done more to change the outlook of child psychology than any other school of thought. To ignore or discredit this work without careful scrutiny and appraisement, would be misguided.

INTRODUCTION

I hope that what I have written in this respect, which is done in all sincerity and from a desire to publicize psycho-analytic doctrines, may be of value to all readers eager to accept their responsibilities in regard to young children seriously.

There is no doubt that the general public is interested in psychology. We have films and novels which have a "psychological angle." The demand for books and lectures on the subject is very great. The response I received to a correspondence course undertaken for men and women in the Forces, from a great variety of backgrounds, was remarkable. Obviously psychology may suffer a little from too much popularization, just as any other science may receive some ridicule and some misunderstanding in this way, but I think it is true nowadays that there are more people prepared to take it seriously and eager to learn more about it. It is to be hoped that this book may serve their needs more fully, for outside America there is no single textbook that covers the whole field of child psychology.

I am greatly indebted to Professor Flugel and to Dr. Susan Isaacs for their skilled and kindly assistance in revising the text of this book. Obviously such a book needs careful editing, and without their help and advice I doubt very much if I should have dared to present this volume of technical child psychology to the general public.

Leicester. *February*, 1948.

SECTION I

RESEARCH IN CHILD PSYCHOLOGY

DURING the present century child psychology has risen to the status of a science. Scientific method has been used in the search for a more accurate knowledge of child development. The work has been carried on in the laboratory and in the nursery, in the consulting room and in the back street. We now know a considerable amount about the normal growth and development of the child, and about both subnormal and abnormal development.

Scientists have studied rats in mazes and monkeys in cages; they have denied dogs their dinners in order to discover the nature of the conditioned reflex, and they have studied babies in cradles in order to discern the true nature of fear.

Some of these methods have been crude and some a little reprehensible. Some at first approach may have seemed a little far-fetched and pseudo-scientific. Statisticians have calculated with great exactitude the presence of certain factors of the mind and the degree of saturation of "g" and "f" and "w." Behaviourists have reconstructed behaviour in terms of electricity, neurologists in terms of neurones and psychoanalysts in terms of oral and anal and genital phases.

It is, however, true to say that nowadays we possess both a more exact and a deeper knowledge of child behaviour than ever before, and much of modern education and child training is based on the scientific findings of modern psychology.

In this summary of research methods and findings, I am not attempting to make an exhaustive survey of all the work undertaken in this field. My purpose is to introduce the reader to the most important researches in child psychology and to outline some of the most significant results. It would be impossible within the scope of the present volume to do justice to the quality or the quantity of this work, but it seems

12 MODERN CHILD PSYCHOLOGY

important to me that the general reader should have some conception of the type and the range of this work. To many people the conclusions of psychologists often seem rather mysterious and rather fantastic. Unless they have some know-ledge of the way by which these conclusions were reached, they are likely to distrust them, and the most solemn statement of a psychologist may be greeted by the remark: "Well, that's only common sense," or "That's quite ridiculous and very far-fetched." My intention is to defend the psychologist from uninformed and hasty criticism, and to present a survey of the literature and some solid facts of well-established knowledge. Many of us who are doing psychological work are concerned not only with its scientific value, but also with the practical effects it may have on our handling of children. A knowledge of child development should help both the parent and the teacher to gain a better understanding of child nature and to modify their attitudes and their methods.

The following is a useful way of classifying the various research methods which have been widely used:

1. The Biographical Method.
2. The Observational Method.
3. The Experimental Method.
4. The Interview Method.
5. The Psychometric Method.
6. The Questionnaire Method.

CHAPTER I

THE BIOGRAPHICAL METHOD

THE first studies of young children, which were undertaken systematically, were in the nature of baby biographies. They were compiled by intelligent observers, usually parents, who took the time and trouble to note down the different stages of the baby's growth and to record the milestones of development. Tiedeman (39), Preyer (30), Scupin (31), Moore (23), Dearborn (10)—to mention some of the best known—were among the first to keep records of the child's development, and their work may be regarded as the foundation of child psychology. These accounts are both delightful and instructive, but they cannot be regarded as entirely reliable data partly because they are in most cases recorded by biased observers, the parents, and partly because their findings refer only to a limited number of children brought up under very favourable conditions. Shinn's (34) account of the development of her young niece is a most useful document of growth, and most pleasing to read. Stern's (36) observations on his own children prove excellent reading, and provide useful documentary evidence. More recently Valentine (40) has added his volume to the writings of psychological parents and his records of his family's development, and his discussion of theoretical arguments are well worth reading. As individual studies they are valuable, but generalizations regarding particular aspects of development cannot be applied to all children because his children were obviously highly intelligent, and brought up in perhaps an optimum environment.

The following observations give a detailed account of speech development which is interesting.

B. (73 days).—Much talking, and smiles when nursing; often he lies and shouts loud and long, happy shouts, apparently from mere exuberance of spirits (37) (p. 396).

14 MODERN CHILD PSYCHOLOGY

E.W. (92 days).—Very active making all sorts of sounds to-day. Coos a great deal to-day, much more than she has ever done, both as regards quantity, quality and variety of sound (loc. cit., p. 397).

B. (7½ mths.).—Repeatedly makes loud quacking noises different from anything heard before (loc. cit., p. 397).

B. (9 mths.).—Delights in making a new guttural sound (loc. cit., p. 397).

B. (1 yr. ½ mth.).—Makes a poor imitation of "bow-bow" (be-be) when I said it while he was looking at dogs in a picture. Looking at picture book B. said "bow-wow" only to dogs (six times) and not to cats (loc. cit., p. 413).

B. (1 yr. 1 mth.).—Noted squeaking like M's mewing at cats' picture, and "bow-wow" at dog's picture (loc. cit., p. 413).

B. (1 yr. 1¾ mths.).—Barks at pictures other than those of dogs (loc. cit., p. 413).

B. (1 yr. 4 mths.).—Sucking sound was used to indicate water almost certainly spontaneously, and "click-clack" instead of occasional "gee-gee." Imitative sounds still made spontaneously when he sees trains, horses, birds, and sheep (loc. cit., p. 413).

Y. (1 yr. 5 mths.).—Oooo . . . bokkle . . . gone . . . bang . . . oooo! (p. 425).

Y. (1 yr. 9½ mths.).—Mummy do ee (it).

Y. (1 yr. 10½ mths.).—Mummy (h)at floor.

B. (1 yr. 11 mths.).—Maba go dere. Mummy 'at floor.

B. (1 yr. 11½ mths.).—Maba ge(t) more bicks.

Y. (2 yrs. 2 mths.).—I know where daddy is. I got comb like daddy's (ibid).

Biographical studies have now been made on a very extensive scale and norms of development, e.g. movement and language, have been established for different age levels. The long-term studies of twins from birth to adolescence undertaken by Berkeley College in America, are very important and valuable as a consistent and scientific account of growth and development over a long period.

The early diary records were the beginning of scientific interest in the subject, and every mother who records the first smile or the first step is herself a scientific observer.

CHAPTER II

THE OBSERVATIONAL METHOD

M A N Y investigators have taken pains to observe a group of children scientifically and have kept careful records of their behaviour.

Shirley (35) has made a useful study of twenty-five normal, well-cared-for infants. She noted, among other characteristics, the marked irritability of the infant in the first few weeks of life, and how *negative* expressional movements and signs of displeasure tend to predominate in early infancy, though this varies with the nature of the environment and probably with inborn temperament.

Shepherd (32) in an unpublished thesis gives an account of a study she made of eight normal healthy infants and their response to the feeding situation. She found among other interesting facts that biting at the breast was commonly noted very early even before the eruption of the teeth.

In Vienna Bühler (6) and her team of investigators made continuous studies of sixty babies and children, both in their homes and in institutions. They recorded the type and nature of sleep, their movement and any form of activity, and their reactions to food over twenty-four-hour periods. Their observations have been recorded carefully and scientifically. Bühler disagreed with laboratory methods as such because she considered they introduced the child to an artificial situation. She preferred to study the child in his own home, or institution, or place familiar to him.

The following table gives an account of the infant's behaviour during the day and night (Reference 7, p. 5).

16 MODERN CHILD PSYCHOLOGY

REACTION GROUPS IN PERCENTAGE OF THE WHOLE DURATION OF THE DAY

Age yr. mths.	Sleep and dozing	Negative reactions	Positive reactions	Spontaneous activity	
0·0	88·7	7·0	3·3	1·0	100%
·3	68·8	12·0	8·2	11·0	100%
·6	56·1	8·4	8·5	27·0	100%
·9	57·0	7·3	7·7	28·0	100%
1·0	55·0	6·4	7·6	31·0	100%

One of the Viennese studies was on the attentivity of young children in play activities. The following result was obtained in regard to *building* play (Reference 7, p. 98).

Age	Duration span
3 yrs.	24 mins.
4 yrs.	22 mins.
5 yrs.	53 mins.
6 yrs.	48 mins.

The tests of development, which are known as the Bühler Baby Tests, cover the child's growth up to five years. They are devised to judge the developmental level of the child under the following "psychological dimensions": intellectual activity, manipulation of material, social responses, learning, body control, sensory perception.

This is Bühler's own classification of "dimensions," and in her scale each item is selected to indicate the child's degree of skill in one or more of these spheres of activity.

The following are test items from the Bühler Developmental Scale for the period one to two years.

One year to one year three months.

Rubs and beats two sticks. (Manipulation of material.)
Stands without support. (Body control.)
Holds object while walking with support. (Body control.)
Understands simple commands. (Social response.)
Can play organized ball game. (Social response.)
Can remember the contents of a box after three minutes. (Intellectual activity.)
Will look for chick (hidden in ball) after three minutes. (Intellectual activity.)

RESEARCH WORK IN CHILD PSYCHOLOGY 17

Will squeeze the ball with the chick. (Learning.)
Can take nest of cubes apart and put it together again. (Manipulation of material.)
Will reach for rusk in a mirror. (Sensory perception.)

One year three months to one year six months.
Can walk. (Body control.)
Can carry object while walking with support. (Body control.)
Observes moving object. (Sensory perception.)
Turns to adult for support. (Social response.)
Understands a prohibition. (Social response.)
Remembers chick and contents of box after eight minutes. (Intellectual activity.)
Imitates beating with drum sticks. (Social response.)
Prefers coloured figures to plain ones. (Sensory perception.)
Can find a rusk under one of two cubes. (Learning.)

One year six months to two years.
Can climb on a chair. (Body control.)
Enjoys social play with a watch. (Social response.)
Names object. (Learning.)
Remembers chick and contents after seventeen minutes. (Intellectual activity.)
Can place two hollow sticks into one another. (Manipulation of material.)
Builds tower of two cubes. (Manipulation of material.)
Contemplates finished structure of grown-ups. (Social response.)
Pulls an object within reach with a stick. (Intellectual activity.)
Recognizes pictures. (Learning.)

The whole scale is fully described in *Testing Children's Development*, by Bühler and Hetzer (8), (published by Allen and Unwin, 1935). It has been used fairly widely in this country and has been found of considerable value.

Nursery schools have proved a fertile field for child observation work both in America and Great Britain.

An important contribution undertaken in this country was

B

18 MODERN CHILD PSYCHOLOGY

that by Isaacs (18) (19). She kept very full records of children in the Malting House School in Cambridge. She studied intellectual development and social and emotional growth in particular. The children were highly intelligent and their activities were largely unrestricted. It provided an ideal setting for making detailed observations of the language and thought of the child, of the inter-play of emotions and of social co-operation and antagonism. Fortunately the records are written up in full in one section, while the interpretative and theoretical matter is included in another. This work is especially significant in that it demonstrates clearly that the very young child is quite capable of logical thought and action, although he may express the results of his thinking and reasoning more readily in a practical than in an abstract way. The second important fact brought out is the intensity and fluctuation of the young child's emotional life and its relation to social development. Many instances of aggressive and sexual behaviour are given showing that feelings of hate and anger and a desire to destroy and to hurt are perfectly normal features of the young child's mental life. His interests in life and death, in biology and in sexual matters are vividly portrayed. Much of the material obtained provides valuable support to psycho-analytic theory, but this will be discussed later.

The following examples quoted from *Social Development in Young Children* provide some evidence of "make-believe aggression" and aggressiveness to newcomers, and to younger children.

Frank made a model of a crocodile showing the spine and the skin markings, the open mouth and the teeth quite plainly. When asked, he said he had seen only a picture of one "on the stairs at home. We have two pictures and one is biting a man's leg off." Later Theobald drew a crocodile with a large mouth which he said "would bite Dan's legs off" (p. 47).

Paul for a time had a long stick as a gun and was "shooting people." Tommy drew a battleship on paper and said to Dan, "I have got a battleship to shoot you with." Dan replied, "Yes. I have one too, and shall shoot you with it," and with quite good humour they "shot" at each other bumping into each other and laughing (p. 47).

RESEARCH WORK IN CHILD PSYCHOLOGY 19

Priscilla came again to school. The boys showed at once a good deal of hostility to her. Dan referred to her as "he," and they talked about cutting her head off, and went into the garden and brought a saw and some shears and approached her in very threatening attitudes (p. 74).

When the children were playing at "giants" in the laurel bush, Paul and Theobald said, "The giant is going to kill Dan," but later they were friendly to him (p. 83).

Frank said he would bite Jessica and tried to make the others join in hurting her. Christopher and Dan went at her and talked of twisting her arms, but soon gave this up when Mrs. I. interfered, as it was only half-hearted and done to please Frank (p. 85).

Such examples could be multiplied indefinitely. They show how naturally children show hostility to others. Other examples show how readily hostility can be changed to friendliness. The deeper sources of love and hate and the child's phantasies and theories about sexuality are discussed at length. These studies of pre-school children behaving in a natural and spontaneous way are extremely valuable and have influenced educational theory and practice to a considerable extent.

When I was teaching in a nursery class in London I found some observational record on each child to be very helpful, and drew up a record form (43) suitable for use in nursery schools which aimed at studying all aspects of development, intellectual, gross motor, language and social-emotional development. The following are the rating sheets of the record form for play observation and emotional development.

PLAY OBSERVATION

What toys does he choose to play with most frequently?

....

....

Is his play mainly with things or with people?

....

....

What form does his play generally take?
Please mark below:

( ) 1. *Free muscular play*, e.g. running, jumping, climbing. (Pleasure in activity for its own sake.)

20   MODERN CHILD PSYCHOLOGY

( ) 2. *Experimental and manipulative*—learning new skills, e.g. trying out kiddy car, hoop, etc., trying to balance, trying out scissors. Working at fitting toys, peg boards, etc. Using sand, plasticine, etc.

( ) 3. *Destructive*, e.g. making things to destroy them; knocking down buildings; using scissors to damage materials; damaging toys.

( ) 4. *Constructive*, e.g. making things for their own sake; building activities, houses, stations, etc.; modelling, painting, drawing, to achieve something.

( ) 5. *Dramatic imitative*, e.g. family play—tea-parties, doll-play, etc. Playing postman, bus conductor, engine-driver, etc.

Record any play incidents you can remember:

EMOTIONAL DEVELOPMENT

(*a*) *General emotional.*

( ) Does he appear contented on the whole?
( ) Does he appear courageous?
( ) Does he try and deal with his own difficulties?
( ) Does he approach new experiences with interest?
( ) Is he normally demonstrative?
( ) Does he conform to restrictions?
( ) Does he appear serene?
( ) Does he appear keen and alert?
( ) Does he seem anxious or worried over trifles?
( ) Does he cry frequently?
( ) Does he tend to evade difficulties?
( ) Does he tend to seek help in difficulties?
( ) Does he show fear in any marked degree when faced with a difficulty?
( ) Does he seem indifferent to any show of affection?
( ) Does he seek affection continually?
( ) Does he tend to exhibit anger when restricted?
( ) Does he get excited easily?
( ) Does he seem indifferent or apathetic?

Have any of the following characteristics been observed?

( ) temper tantrums,
( ) nail biting,

RESEARCH WORK IN CHILD PSYCHOLOGY 21

( ) lip sucking and biting,
( ) nose-picking,
( ) hair-pulling,
( ) manipulation of genitalia,
( ) thigh rubbing or wriggling,
( ) facial grimaces (frequently),
( ) wetting during play, ( ) during rest,
( ) stuttering or any form of speech defect,
( ) regressive tendencies—(seeking always to be the baby, climbing into doll's pram, wrapping self up, etc.).
Have any specific fears been observed?
( ) animals,
( ) strangers,
( ) stories, e.g. *Little Black Sambo*,
( ) dirt (sand, mud or water—shown as disgust),
( ) mess (plasticine, paint or paste—shown as disgust),
( ) worms,
( ) toy guns,
( ) noise,
( ) W.C. plug or water.
Note any if not included in this list.

In America, Bridges (5) has made a careful study of social behaviour and has traced the stages as follows:

Aloofness and indifference; aggressiveness and unfriendliness; social co-operation.

Her account of emotional development is not so fortunate in the light of recent studies. She contends that the first emotional expression is general excitement, and that all later emotions are gradually derived from that. Distress and delight develop in infancy, and anger and fear at two years of age. Her final differentiation is as follows:

Shame, fear, anxiety.
Jealousy, anger, envy and disappointment.
Disgust and distress.
Excitement.
Delight, elation, joy and hope.
Affection (parental and filial).

I do not think this picture of the emotional life of the

22 MODERN CHILD PSYCHOLOGY

young child is accurate. Quite distinct emotions of anger, fear and jealousy can be detected in the first year of life. The psychoanalysts give a very different account, and, though less generally acceptable, it is, I think, nearer the truth.

Bridges also drew up certain rating scales of social behaviour and standardized them widely. The following one is a useful method of assessing social adjustment.

SOCIAL BEHAVIOUR SCALE
K.M.B. BRIDGES.
(SCHOOL)

Name .... *Date of Birth*............
Address .... *Age* ....
School .... *Rater's Name*............
Class ....

DIRECTIONS

This rating scale refers to the child's behaviour in school during the last six months, and should be marked by the teacher or the psychologist after consultation with the teacher.

Mark (2) for each statement which applies correctly, and (0) for each item which does not apply correctly to the child under consideration. Mark (1) if the statement only partly or sometimes applies, and in all cases of doubt. Do not miss any item.

Multiply the total score by $\frac{3}{2}$ to obtain the final score for each child.

SCORE

1 .... Plays amicably with other children without mischief making.
2 .... Does not hold aloof or prefer to play alone.
3 .... Co-operates agreeably in school or class activities.
4 .... Is not easily led into breaking rules or naughty pranks.
5 .... Plays fair and follows rules at games.
6 .... Tries to keep order and control unruly playmates.
7 .... Does not lead others into trouble or mischief.
8 .... Does not disturb and interfere with others.
9 .... Is considerate and helpful to other children.
10 .... Is not noisy or talkative, demanding attention in class.

RESEARCH WORK IN CHILD PSYCHOLOGY

11 .... Does not fidget or get out of seat in class.
12 .... Does not steal money.
13 .... Seldom disobeys orders and is not defiant.
14 .... Is not insolent to teachers.
15 .... Is not surly or resentful when corrected.
16 .... Is gentle and not rough with smaller children.
17 .... Does not try to dominate others.
18 .... Does not act violently in temper when crossed or thwarted.
19 .... Does not quarrel or start fights.
20 .... Does not allow himself to be bullied or put upon.
21 .... Is not cruel to animals.
22 .... Does not steal objects other than money.
23 .... Does not cheat in lessons.
24 .... Does not tell tales of others to get them into trouble.
25 .... Does not tell boastful lies or fanciful "stories."
26 .... Does not play truant.
27 .... Does not come late to school.
28 .... Does not cry easily or cease effort in face of difficulty.
29 .... Is not destructive of school property.
30 .... Usually works with diligence.
31 .... Usually does clean and tidy work.
32 .... Does not show undesirable sex behaviour.
33 .... Does not tell evasive lies or try to deceive.

———

Total.

———

Final Score.   Docile Rank........

Comments:

Other studies of nursery schoolchildren have been made at the Merrill-Palmer School, Detroit, at the Yale Psycho-Clinic, New Haven, at Iowa and Minnesota, and at many other centres.

The Merrill-Palmer School, is a most valuable institute of child psychology with two large nursery schools where students can train and study. Very thorough child studies are made on diet, nutrition, health and physical development as well as on intellectual and social-emotional development.

24   MODERN CHILD PSYCHOLOGY

At Yale, Gesell (11) has done an immense amount of valuable research which I will report in more detail later. The nursery school is on the ground floor of the Institute of Human Relations at Yale. In the same building on upper floors all types and varieties of psychological research are being carried on; rats are being studied in mazes, psycho-pathic patients in observation wards, chimpanzees are kept on the roof and their learning behaviour investigated while legions of statisticians, stenographers and cinematographers' operators keep careful records. In the nursery school a one-way vision screen permits students to observe the children without themselves being seen.

Blatz and Bott (2 and 3) are other American psychologists who have studied the behaviour of children in the nursery school extensively, and published their findings.

Some schools of thought in America have become rather self-conscious about psychology, and have perhaps reduced it in some respects to an absurdity. They lay great emphasis for instance, on habit training, and the importance of establishing good habits early, especially in relation to eating and sleeping and eliminating. To insist on a rigid routinized procedure, as is done in some American nurseries, is too restricting to a child. The value of a routine is widely recognized, but it is equally important to be able to depart from it occasionally, and habits carefully inculcated by painstaking means can be upset overnight by some emotional disturbance.

Some reference must be made to Murphy's (24) work. She made a very comprehensive study of sympathy in young children from long-term observations in a nursery school. The term sympathy is used in a wide sense, and may be defined as "the capacity of individual human beings to interpret and respond to the behaviour of other human beings. It is intimately connected with all the other responses of a friendly and constructive nature that are the foundation of a co-operative society." It thus includes a wide variety of co-operative, friendly and sympathetic responses to other children and adults. The focal point selected for study is the analysis of children's responses to distress in other children. She devised a rating

RESEARCH WORK IN CHILD PSYCHOLOGY 25

scale for sympathy and related behaviour which includes items such as the following: (p. 329)

'Imitates another child's words while playing. Takes away another child's toy. Defends rights of smaller child. Joins attack on one child by another. Tells child not to cry. Teases new child. Pummels child who falls accidentally. Cries when hears the crying of another child not in sight. Laughs when hearing another child laugh. Warns another child of danger. Gets toy to give to child in place of wanted toy. Tells child "I don't like you," or equivalent. Asks child if hurt after fall. Asks child why he is crying.'

The rating scale, which consisted of some forty-four items, was completed for the group of children being observed and ranked according to a five-point scale. Similarly, pictures, animals, stories, questions and certain laboratory situations, e.g. a baby in a play-pen, were used to elicit sympathetic responses. Some of her general conclusions are interesting.

We saw how the specific features of each aspect of personality were intimately interwoven with other aspects. Aggression, sympathetic responses, intelligence and fears do not occur like books on a shelf, but the internal character of each conditions the other in specific ways. The outstanding example of this was the use of defence techniques for the sympathetic assistance of other children by children who were aggressive (p. 280).

Again:

Each child's configuration of personality traits is different from the other, and where one child may have a high rank on aggression, sympathy, co-operation and imagination, another child may have a high rank on one and a low rank on the others. Some constellations look like predominantly social or predominantly self-centred patterns, but even if types like this do exist they tell us nothing about the organization of behaviour tendencies within the type (p. 282).

She finds from her results that there is a consistent correlation of 0·40[1], or thereabouts, between aggressive and sympathetic behaviour—which points to the importance of a

[1] The correlation coefficient is a measure of the amount of agreement between two ranks. It ranges from + 1·0 to − 1·0 and can thus be positive or negative.

26 MODERN CHILD PSYCHOLOGY

general tendency toward outgoing responses, underlying both aggressive and sympathetic behaviour (p. 282). This agrees with Bott's concept of general emotionality (known as "e") derived from a study of older children and of adults.

In America there appears to be more time and more money for research. In *Personality Development in Childhood* (42) a collection of monographs of the Society for Research in Child Development (Volume I), an exhaustive account of research work undertaken in America is given and a summary of the findings included.

The following are some of the subjects chosen for research:

Crying
Fear } in infancy.
Anger
Jealousy

Social activity
Negativism } in the pre-school period.
Laughter
Language

Emotional Adjustment in the Schoolchild. Children's Interests and Attitudes in Regard to Books, Movies, Play, Vocations, Politics. Racial Characteristics. Twins. The Only Child. Intelligence. Personality Traits.

I will give a brief summary of the research findings obtained by a large number of investigators.

> The picture of *Infancy* in terms of research findings is predominantly one of change; change from diffuse activity to adaptive activity behaviour, from meagre stimulus-response functioning to integrated responses in the light of total situational aspects. The infant is described as an organism who can respond positively or negatively toward a limited number and kind of factors in his environment. Commonly he responds to discomfort, restricted movements, and loud sounds by reacting negatively—crying, thrashing, flushing, puckering his face. Approach responses are expressed by expansive movements, smiles, sucking movements and the like. . . .
> By the end of the second year such terms as anger, fear, joy, disgust, jealousy are used to describe the child's behaviour, indicating differential responses to stimuli (loc. cit., p. 15).

RESEARCH WORK IN CHILD PSYCHOLOGY 27

Blanton, Bridges, Goodenough, Shirley, Washburne and Watson have done particularly important work on this period of child development.

In the *pre-school period*,
the child acquires a capacity for more social activity and for more maturity in his social attitudes. He learns to co-operate more readily, to respect other property rights in some small measure, to lead or follow a leader as the occasion demands. He is apt to be negative in certain situations, but to overcome this in large measure by the end of his fourth year. He is apt to laugh most in social surroundings, and to find more abstract and more complicated situations mirthful as he grows older. He comes to employ language more as a means of communicating his ideas and his wishes to other persons than as a means of "thinking out loud" (loc. cit., p. 49).

The names of Blatz, Bott, Bridges, Gesell, Goodenough, Parten and Washburne are connected with important work during this period.

The young *schoolchild* continues to exhibit growth in social and emotional patterns, but the rate of development is slower and perhaps for this reason less emphasis has been placed upon the period. Although the child in the first grade can maintain leadership only in a small group, makes little distinction between the sexes in choosing friends, and has little aptitude for evaluating his friends' abilities, by the time he has reached the sixth grade he may exhibit a quality of leadership which enables him to sway an entire classroom group, is likely to show a decided preference for friends of the same sex, and will be able to distinguish among his classmates at least those with outstanding abilities and characteristics.

The movies, books and the radio make profound impressions which are in turn reflected in his play behaviour and attitudes. Vocational ambitions are likely to be impractical and wish fulfilling (loc. cit., p. 84).

With the *older schoolchild* development is again accelerated. Interest in the opposite sex blossoms at this period, with all the accompanying interest in dress, parties, dancing and the like. Unisexual groups lose their appeal, and individual creative interests tend to diminish. The girl responds to this new appeal earlier

28 MODERN CHILD PSYCHOLOGY

than the boy. The individual who fails to conform to the group is apt to be more isolated than at any other period in childhood (loc. cit., p. 85).

Downey, Lehman, Pressey, Terman and Witty have done some interesting work on child development during this period.

CHAPTER III

THE EXPERIMENTAL METHOD

P E R H A P S the best-known psychologists who have utilized experimental methods are Watson (41) and Gesell (11).

Watson, the well-known behaviourist, claims to study child psychology in a truly objective way. He insisted on recording behaviour exactly, without interpretation or subjective suggestions. He studied infants closely to detect the true nature of instinctive behaviour. He studied fear and anger and love responses, and claimed that fear was instinctive only at the experience of a sudden loss of support or the sound of a loud noise, anger in relation only to restriction of movement, and love only in relation to fondling or petting. His work was an attempt to prove the theory of reflexes and he founded what is known as the Behaviourist School of Psychology. He fails, however, to take into account the *whole situation* as it appears to the child, and to recognize the value or meaningfulness of a particular experience to a child. Moreover he denies and disregards the influence of unconscious impulses.

His classic experiments are so well known that a brief description here may be of interest to the lay reader.

He first observed that a sudden loud noise and a sudden loss of support were the only sure stimuli to produce a reaction of fear. He noted that they invariably resulted in a sudden catching of breath, marked changes in the heart beat and respiratory rhythm, crying and throwing upward of the hands.

He then arranged for the baby to be presented with a favourite toy or pet animal while simultaneously a steel bar was struck. Instantly the child was seen to stiffen, to catch its breath, cry and then crawl away. After a few repetitions of this experiment, the infant reacted to the neutral object, the toy or animal, with fear as it would react to the loud noise, *although no noise was actually made.* This is known as a con-

30 MODERN CHILD PSYCHOLOGY

ditioned emotional reaction. Similarly he proved that a child could be conditioned to fear, darkness, a flash of lightning, a furry animal and many other things.

He further went on to show that it was possible to recondition a child. The baby was given his dinner while at the same time a pet rabbit of whom the baby had been taught to be afraid, was disclosed at the far end of the room. The next time the rabbit was brought a little nearer to what was called the "point of tolerance." At the end of a few weeks the baby would allow the rabbit to sit on the table or even in its arms while his dinner was presented to him, and showed no outward sign of fear.

Gesell (11) (12) (13) (14) (15) has also done most important pioneer work, and his writings and findings are studied by every serious student of child psychology. He made detailed studies of infants and utilized for the purpose a careful laboratory method—a specially designed photographic dome made of one-way vision screening whereby the observer could observe and record movements and behaviour while remaining unobserved. He made careful studies of all aspects of development, e.g. reaching, grasping, handling, hand preference, motor co-ordination and the like. He made records of vocalization and locomotion. The result of many thousand observations on a great number of infants over many years produced the Gesell Developmental Scale, which is virtually the earliest form of a standardized intelligence test. The norms of gross motor development, fine motor co-ordination, adaptive behaviour, language and personal social development were established for the normal child at each month of his life from birth up to three years and later. His studies of twins are particularly valuable. His account of maturation and the effect of environment is most useful. His records of subnormal and supernormal children provide important clinical material.

Probably Gesell has done more to build up reliable norms of normal development than any other investigator.

The following is a summary of developmental items included at *the sixth month level.*

(M = motor development. P = personal-social behaviour. A = adaptive behaviour. L = language development.)

RESEARCH WORK IN CHILD PSYCHOLOGY 31

Ratings represent the following frequency: A+ = 1% — 19%. A = 20% — 49%. B+ = 50% — 64%. B = 65% — 84%. C = 85% — 100.%)

MOTOR DEVELOPMENT
Holds head erect, C.
Sits slight support, B+. Alone, A+.
Rolls back to stomach, B.
Creeps or hitches, A+.
Makes stepping movements, A.
Hands react to table, C.
Inhibits head and one hand, B. Manipulates with one hand, A.
Secures pellet whole hand, A. Fine prehension, A+.
Picks up cube, B.
Holds two objects, B. Drops one for third, B+.
Releases objects: throws to floor A, drops into cup (imitation) A.
Preference one hand, A+.
Splashes in tub, B.

PERSONAL-SOCIAL BEHAVIOUR
Shows consciousness of strangers, B.
Pats table, B.
Bangs spoon, B.
Turns head to bell, B.
Reacts mirror image, A.
Expresses recognition, B.
Frolics when played with, B+.
Plays with objects, C.
Casts objects for noise, A.
Reacts to music; stops crying, B; coos, A; smiling, laughing, B+.
Takes bottle in and out of mouth, A.

ADAPTIVE BEHAVIOUR
Manipulates spoon, cup and saucer, B. Exploratory manipulations, A.
Reaches directly spoon, B.

32   MODERN CHILD PSYCHOLOGY

Blinks at pencil, B.

Regards cube, C. Regards pellet, B+.

Lifts inverted cup, B. Secures cube, A+.

Fallen object: conscious, B; looks for, A+.

Dangling ring: closes in, C; clasps, B; above head, B+; persistent reaching, A.

Paper: crumples, B; purposeful reaction, A.

LANGUAGE DEVELOPMENT

Says mama, dada, or equivalent syllables, A+.

It is thus clear from this data that almost all children can hold their heads erect at six months, most children can turn their heads at the sound of a bell, and very few children can say definite syllables at this age. This list gives a very detailed summary of the repertoire of a six-months-old baby. Gesell's scale has been widely used, and is especially valuable in assessing developmental level in cases of adoption.

It is necessary to make some reference to the School of Gestalt Psychology, because it has had considerable influence on psychological thinking in general. The findings of this school have been fully discussed and explained by Professor Koffka.[1]

The term "gestalt" means shape, form, or organization. The followers of this school are at pains to show that all our sensations, perceptions and conceptions are the result of organization. "What happens to a part of the whole is determined by inherent laws in the whole." The context, the associations, the links with other phenomena determines the nature of our sensations, perceptions and conceptions. Memory is not a mere entity or function, but the result and the determiner of organized processes. Traces are left behind which influence our way of behaving and thinking.

"This is a dynamic theory in which the processes organize themselves under the prevailing dynamic and constraining conditions." This theory is especially important when applied to the perceptual field. What we perceive is influenced by what is contiguous or contrasting to it, its distinctness and

[1]Koffka F. *The Principles of Gestalt Psychology*, Kegan Paul, 1935.

RESEARCH WORK IN CHILD PSYCHOLOGY 33

shape in relation to other shapes, its segregation and separateness from other objects in the visual field. All kinds of interesting experiments about the perception of shape, of points, of lines, of colour, and of sound have been undertaken. It was found that we tend to organize our perceptions to produce a meaningful shape. This is especially applicable to the infant's development of perception and his way of learning about the world around him.

Learning is based on laws of organization inherent in the mind, and is essentially dynamic, not a mere mechanical linking of associations.

The method of *successive comparison* is outlined in some detail. This influences the learning process in that a person compares a particular perception with successive perceptions, and the preceding perception influences the present one. What has gone before influences the present, and a process of inter-relationship and inter-communication takes place. The mind seeks always to organize its experiences into wholes, into meaningful unities. The whole process is essentially dynamic and active. The background, the context, the associations are of great importance and no behaviour must be considered as an isolated unit.

A child who has an exciting experience after being exposed to a very dull and uneventful environment will be more strongly affected by the experience than if he was constantly enjoying it.

A child will react more strongly to a bright light in a dark room, than a bright light in a room full of light.

A child will not experience such intense fear if his mother is holding him when a peal of thunder is heard or a fierce dog barks.

Much of the Gestalt psychology is difficult and technical, and needs careful reading. The general principles are, however, very important.

C

CHAPTER IV

THE INTERVIEW METHOD

P I A G E T (25—29) is a psychologist who has provoked much stimulating controversy and his methods and findings are of considerable importance.

He undertook to study the nature of child thinking, and was at pains to demonstrate that it differed essentially from adult thinking. His method was to interview each child, to ask numerous questions about causality and natural phenomena for instance, in the hope of elucidating the child's method of thinking and power of reasoning. This "clinical method" was an artificial one in that it presented the child with an unfamiliar and rather irksome situation, and the questions asked were concerning phenomena with which the child had had but meagre acquaintance, e.g. "How did the sun begin?" "Does the sun move?" "What are dreams?" "Is this fly alive? Why?" In such a situation a child is out of his depth. Rather than admit that he is nonplussed he will invent an answer, or fall back on more primitive conceptions and give semi-magical or animistic explanations. Very young children think largely in personal terms, and tend to regard objects in the external world as having the same feelings and powers as themselves. A belief in animism is characteristic of primitive peoples, and until the child has had sufficient experience of the real world to check his naïve personal viewpoint, which is similar in some respects to primitive folk, he will tend to use animistic explanations. This does not mean that he cannot think quite logically concerning matters which have come within his own experience.

Piaget outlines certain definite stages of child thinking. He claims that the mental life of the child is characterized by the following developmental phases:

Autistic thinking (phantasy thought); Egocentrism (implicit belief in his own ideas).

RESEARCH WORK IN CHILD PSYCHOLOGY 35

His talking during this second stage is in the nature of a *collective monologue* in which he talks mainly to himself. Piaget contends that there is no real interchange of ideas. The child cannot handle judgments of such relations as brother-sister, or right-left involving reciprocity at this stage. The first period of *logical unification* does not take place until seven years in his view. And he does not consider a child capable of real logical thought until about the age of eleven or twelve years.

He appears to ignore the fact that a young child can give a practical demonstration of how to make green paint out of blue and yellow, how he makes his bicycle to go, or the effect of heat on such substances as wax or wood or water—that is when the phenomena is within the range of his experience. Hazlitt, Isaacs, and Mead (22) have presented evidence to refute some of Piaget's theories from their study of the behaviour of pre-school children and primitive children. It is clear that young children who possess only a limited vocabulary seek a manipulative solution to a problem rather than a verbal one, and use the logic of action rather than the logic of speech.

It is equally clear, as Piaget himself points out, that animistic thought is co-existent with logical thought, but this is also apparent in the case of adults when faced with a novel or difficult situation. People tend to let personal feelings intrude and influence impersonal situations. They blame circumstances, and endow situations and objects with personal emotions when they are at a loss or annoyed or confused, e.g. "the fire will never burn for me," or "the train is sure to be late if I am in a hurry."

Piaget considers that it is in the first appearance of the "social instincts" at about seven or eight years that the key to intellectual development lies. Before this, he contends, the child is egocentric and uncritical. From self-criticism, logical judgment and ability to reason is born. Modern psychology is critical of this point of view in regard to the sudden maturation of the "social instincts." Clearly they are the outcome of a gradual growth process from quite early infancy when the infant begins to learn to adapt to society. Moreover impact of,

36 MODERN CHILD PSYCHOLOGY

and contact with the physical world, forces a child to abandon his phantasies and to re-adapt his behaviour. The observations of young children undertaken by Isaacs (18) for instance, indicates quite clearly to my mind that they are capable of original thought, practical and verbal solutions, some verbal formulations and even discussions.

Here is a delightful example quoted from *The Intellectual Growth in Young Children*, which illustrates this point.

> Denis (3 yrs. 9 mths.). "The bread's buttered already, isn't it? So if we want it without butter we can't, can we?—unless we 'crape it off with a knife, and if we want it without butter and don't want to 'crape it off wiv' a knife, we have to eat it with butter, don't we?" (p. 65).

Again:

> Ursula (4 yrs.). "Why are there two l's in pull? We don't need two, do we? One would do, wouldn't it?" (One is reminded of Bernard Shaw's recent letter to *The Times* when he questions the necessity of having a "b" at the end of bomb.) (p. 84.)

In my own nursery class the discussion held by three four-year-olds quoted in *The Natural Development of the Child* (4) is relevant to this point (p. 43).

> Jean and Janet, aged four, said, "Let's have a caravan and go away and away. Wheels and a chimney, too! But just us two. No one else."
>
> Jill: "I'd come, too."
>
> Jean and Janet: "No you wouldn't. We shouldn't let you."
>
> Jill: "I'd come in the door."
>
> Jean and Janet: "We'd bolt the door."
>
> Jill: "Well, I should come in the window."
>
> Jean and Janet: "No. We'd bolt the window."
>
> Jill: "Well, I should break the window."
>
> Jean and Janet: "No. You couldn't. We should bar the window."
>
> Jill gave up at this point.

Certainly some of Piaget's writings are well worth studying, but his somewhat extreme view on the nature of child thought is not generally supported by other psychologists.

RESEARCH WORK IN CHILD PSYCHOLOGY 37

Anthony's (1) work on *The Child's Discovery of Death* is interesting, and her methods of investigation are similar in some respects to those of Piaget. By means of interviews, intelligence tests, absurdity tests, and story completion tests she made a study of some 117 children to try to determine the nature of their conception of death. The following are some of her results:

1. The child is liable to feel a strong *sense* of *guilt* when a member of his family dies. This sense of guilt will almost certainly be, from a common-sense point of view, utterly unreasonable (1) (p. 196).
2. The idea of death occurs readily in children's phantasy thinking.
3. The idea arises as a response to suggestions of grief and fear, the grief being frequently associated by the child with loss or separation, and the fear with aggressive intrusion.
4. Phantasy about death is commonly found together with talion ideas (retaliation and reparation) (1) (p. 206).
Ben (aged 6 yrs.). "Do you think when we die we go up to the shops in heaven, and then God buys us and puts us in the larder and eats us (1) (p. 131).
And Richard (aged 5 yrs. 5 mths.). "We shall go up in the sky if a war come so you needn't mind. The angels will let down a long rope with a hook on the end and catch you up on the hook and then you'll turn into an angel, and it will be lovely 'cos you'll be able to fly—because angels can fly, they have wings" (1) (p. 131).

The records include many delightful and naïve childish ideas about death:

Griffiths (17) made a study of imagination in young children by a modified form of the interview method coupled with *projection methods*. She gave twenty interviews of twenty to forty minutes duration to fifty five-year-old children, thirty attending London elementary and twenty attending State schools in Brisbane. She listened to their free conversation, to a spontaneous story, to their account of their dreams or day dreams, and studied their drawings and their comments on them, their reactions to an ink blot test and to an imagery test. Each child was also given a mental test.

38 MODERN CHILD PSYCHOLOGY

She distinguished two main types of emotional reaction to environment, (1) emotions accompanying *success*, positive in type and showing self-confidence, satisfaction, pride and love of objects, and (2) emotions accompanying *failure*, negative in type and showing disappointment, humiliation, fear and hatred of objects. She also found evidence of marked ambivalence (loving and hating) towards significant persons, and marked expression of antagonism towards persons, in play, in free phantasy, day dreams, and dreams.

CHAPTER V

THE PSYCHOMETRIC METHOD

T H E scales devised by Bühler and Gesell have already been described in these pages. They are in the nature of psychometric methods. Stutsman (37) has also devised some very useful and practical tests for children between the ages of eighteen months and five years. She does not attempt to study the whole development of the child, but only his level of intelligence as judged by his ability to solve certain practical problems. These tests which are to some extent the adaptation and inclusion of such well-known tests as the Manikin, the Wallin Peg Boards, the Seguin form board, consist of a battery of puzzles and games which are intrinsically interesting to the child. Matching colours, fitting pegs into holes, boxes into a nest, shapes into their insets or matching pictures and completing jigsaws—all these performance tests have been tried out and carefully standardized as being particularly suitable for a certain age level. The child's score is based on the time taken and the correctness of the solution. The type of performance required is similar to that enjoyed by a normal child in a nursery school, and usually the child enters into the test with zest and enthusiasm.

Of course it is not wise to assume that an assessment of intelligence, especially at this age level, is entirely reliable. At best it is a measure of his effective level of intelligence, and not necessarily his optimum. Emotional attitude, social responsiveness, general anxiety, for instance, may prejudice his performance. But an estimate of mental age or developmental level on such a scale as the Merrill-Palmer, as this is called, gives a useful indication of intellectual ability.

The Terman-Merrill Scale (38) is probably the best known and the most widely used in Child Guidance Clinics and by School Medical Officers. These tests are a revision and an

THE MANIKIN

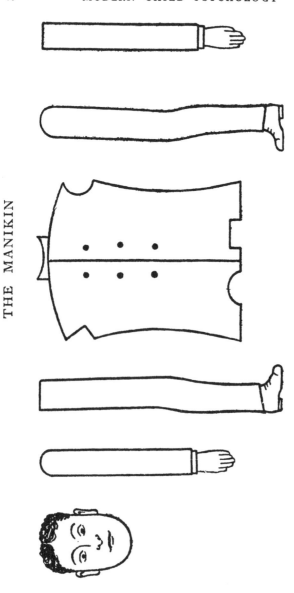

The child is asked to put the pieces together. He is not told what they are meant to represent. He is expected to place the rounded leg and arm in the rounded insets and the square-ended leg and arm in their appropriate places, and put the head in its right place. A partially correct solution scores some marks, but the whole has to be fitted correctly together to gain a full score.

THE SEGUIN BOARD

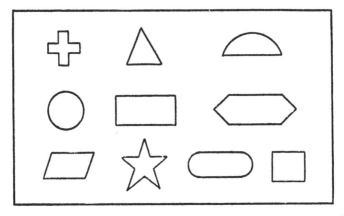

In this test the child has to replace the wooden insets into their correct places in the form board. Speed and correctness of performances are scored, and number of errors counted.

THE WALLIN PEG BOARDS

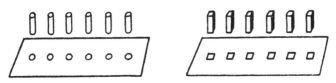

The child is asked to replace the round pegs in the round holes and the square pegs in the square holes as quickly as possible.

42 MODERN CHILD PSYCHOLOGY

improvement on the original Binet tests. They include many simple performance tests suitable for very young children, are very well standardized, and are especially reliable for school children. They are standardized for children of eighteen months of age to superior adult level.

The following are the test items which a six-year-old of normal intelligence is expected to be able to pass:

1. Knows the meaning of five words such as orange, envelope, straw, puddle, tap, eyelash, roar, scorch.
2. Can reproduce a bead chain from memory which consists of square and round beads alternatively.
3. Can detect four out of five missing features from incomplete pictures, e.g. a barrow without a wheel, a rabbit without an ear, a boot without a lace, a tea-pot without a handle, and a glove without a finger.
4. Can count out three, nine, five, seven, etc. bricks on request. (Three correct out of five.)
5. Can distinguish differences from likeness when presented pictorially, e.g. a round shape from square shapes, a black circle from white circles, when asked to show the one that is not the same as the others.
6. Can show the shortest way for a boy to go to school on a simple maze form. (Two out of three correct.)

Such tests are easy to administer and a good response can readily be elicited from most children.

Recently Valentine[1] has undertaken a useful piece of work in devising an intelligence scale suitable for children between the ages of eighteen months and eleven years based on a combination of the most satisfactory and reliable tests devised by Gesell, Porteous, Burt, Terman, and from the Merrill-Palmer Scale. He claims that by including a large number and a great variety of tests the scale is intrinsically interesting to the child and more reliable. He purposefully makes the instructions as simple and as brief as possible, and the scale involves the use of very simple apparatus and material which is easily obtainable in order that teachers can make full use of the tests themselves. He assumes that intelligence testing of this simple type can

[1]Valentine, C. W. *Intelligence Tests for Young Children*. Methuen, 1945.

RESEARCH WORK IN CHILD PSYCHOLOGY 43

readily be undertaken by the teacher and claims that these tests "are primarily meant to afford a preliminary estimate of the general stage of development." He considers the results for children of four years and over to be the most reliable, as the tests were given to a greater number of children than in the case of those suitable for children under four.

The scale is especially useful in the infant and junior departments and is suitable for placing the pupils "in a fairly reliable order of merit, to select those of superior and those of dull intelligence, and to give a preliminary selection of possible mental defectives."

Although there is little that is original in this scale, the combination of well-tried tests in one battery is a valuable and a novel one.

It is outside the scope of this book to give a full account of the tremendous amount of work that has been done in recent years in mental testing. The references at the end will introduce the reader to other literature that explains the different measures of intelligence in detail.

CHAPTER VI

THE QUESTIONNAIRE METHOD

T H E use of questionnaires in an attempt to elicit the opinions of children, parents, teachers and others on various subjects, is a common practice. Obviously it is open to criticism in that the subjects are liable to misrepresent their opinions, and are usually biased in their own favour. However, some useful information can be obtained by this means. Cummings[1] recently made a study of the incidence of emotional symptoms in school children between the ages of two and seven + years. A number of teachers were asked to observe 239 children in three large infant schools. A random sample was obtained by going through the registers and picking out every second child. The teachers then completed a record form. It was found that the following emotional symptoms had the highest incidence for the whole group.

	%
Excitability and restlessness	28·9
Day-dreaming, lack of concentration or laziness	28·9
Generalized anxiety, timidity or shyness	23·0
Specific fears	22·2
Bladder control, frequency of micturition	21·3
Nervous habits	18·0

Aggressiveness, cruelty, day-dreaming and obstinacy were found more frequently in boys than in girls.

Incontinence and frequency of micturition decreased with age.

Specific fears tended to decline with age, also such comfort habits as thumb-sucking, sucking bricks, etc.

Day-dreaming and lack of concentration appeared to

[1]Cummings. *The Incidence of Emotional Symptoms in Young Children.* Brit. J. Ed. Psy., Vol. XIV, Pt. III, November, 1944.

RESEARCH WORK IN CHILD PSYCHOLOGY 45

increase with age, probably because more formal work is included and less free play in the time-table.

"Over-protected" children showed more "nervous" symptoms than "neglected" children. "Neglected" children tended to be more anti-social, more aggressive or cruel or dishonest.

The results are interesting and suggest the need for more adjustment classes, using play methods in the infant departments.

Jenkinson (20) made a valuable study of children's reading preferences and habits in this way. He obtained replies from 2,900 children (936 secondary school boys and 719 secondary school girls, and 634 senior school boys and 611 senior school girls, between twelve and fifteen years of age).

The following are some of his results:

BOYS
SECONDARY

Age	School Stories	Detective	Home Life	Adventure	Love	Historical	Collections Annuals	Technical
	%	%	%	%	%	%	%	%
12 +	14	7·8	11·5	42·8	—	—	8·1	—
13 +	10	15·4	14·9	41·8	—	—	—	—
14 +	6·7	17·6	8·3	39·9	—	6·1	—	6·7
15 +	5·3	18·2	—	36·2	6·8	9·6	—	9·8

SENIOR

Age	School Stories	Detective	Home Life	Adventure	Love	Historical	Collections Annuals	Technical
12 +	12·2	5·2	7·5	53·3	—	6·6	7·1	—
13 +	12·4	6·7	7·3	34·6	—	5·4	5·1	—
14 +	11·5	7·8	11·5	51·6	—	—	7·2	—

GIRLS
SECONDARY

Age	School Stories	Detective	Home Life	Adventure	Love	Humour	Historical	Collections
	%	%	%	%	%	%	%	%
12 +	22·3	—	33·5	17·6	7·9	—	6·1	5·6
13 +	16·6	10·0	23·0	22·3	12·6	—	—	5·0
14 +	12·4	10·0	18·0	24·7	16·9	—	8·7	—
15 +	—	11·8	15·5	22·5	19·6	6·3	13·3	—

SENIOR

Age	School Stories	Detective	Home Life	Adventure	Love	Humour	Historical	Collections
12 +	24·9	—	30·0	21·8	5·8	—	—	11·6
13 +	26·3	—	26·8	20·2	7·6	—	5·7	9·4
14 +	23·2	—	25·5	16·2	11·4	—	9·6	9·2

46 MODERN CHILD PSYCHOLOGY

Girls give more time to reading school stories, love stories, and stories of home life, while boys enjoy adventure and detective stories more.

An analysis of Youth Centre interests was made by Hammond[1] on 140 boys and girls of *sixteen* years. Sports and physical activities are the most popular. The data gave evidence of an athletic type and a more sedentary type preferring artistic and intellectual interests. The girls tended to belong to the latter type and the boys to the former.

The order of popularity of the activities, expressed as the percentage of the whole group claiming interest in them was as follows:—

	Boys	Girls	Staying Group (four or more attendances)	Leaving Group less than four attendances)	Total
Table tennis	85	95	90	90	90
Darts	84	61	74	71	73
Billiards	81	11	45	52	48
Cycling	78	80	81	77	79
Dancing	74	91	81	83	82
Swimming	73	82	78	75	77
Physical training	73	67	69	71	70
Camping	73	80	76	77	77
Quiet games	57	58	58	56	57
"Keep Fit"	50	74	64	58	62
Rambling	49	82	65	63	64
Reading	32	42	39	35	37
Discussion	31	41	36	35	36
Dramatics	28	76	46	59	51
Hobbies	27	36	27	38	31
Netball	11	82	43	46	44

Many other investigators have used the questionnaire method and there are many useful reports of studies undertaken on similar lines reported in the literature. I have referred only

[1]Hammond, W. H. *An Analysis of Youth Centre Interests.* B. J. Ed. Psy., Vol. XV, Pt. III, 1945.

RESEARCH WORK IN CHILD PSYCHOLOGY 47

to three recent studies giving interesting results at three different age levels.

This general survey of the research work undertaken in the field of child psychology is perhaps sufficient to indicate to the general reader that a great amount of useful work has been done, and a great variety of method employed. The list of references at the end of this section will, I hope, tempt the serious student to read more as it is impossible to give detailed accounts within the scope of this volume.

REFERENCES.

1.	Anthony, S.	*The Child's Discovery of Death*	Kegan Paul, 1940
2.	Blatz, W. E. & Bott, H.	*Parents and the Pre-School Child*	Dent, 1928
3.	Blatz, W. E. & Bott, H.	*The Management of Young Children*	Dent, 1931
4.	Bowley, A. H.	*The Natural Development of the Child*	Livingstone, 1940
5.	Bridges, K. M.	*Social and Emotional Development of the Pre-School Child*	Kegan Paul, 1931
6.	Bühler, C.	*The First Year of Life*	Day, 1930
7.	Bühler, C.	*From Birth to Maturity*	Kegan Paul, 1931
8.	Bühler, C. & Hetzer, H.	*Testing Children's Development*	Allen & Unwin, 1935
9.	Cattell, R. B.	*A Guide to Mental Testing*	Univ. of London Press, 1936
10.	Dearborn	*Motor-Sensory Development*	Baltimore, 1910
11.	Gesell, A.	*The Mental Growth of the Pre-School Child*	Macmillan, 1925
12.	Gesell, A.	*Infancy and Human Growth*	Macmillan, 1928
13.	Gesell, A.	*The Guidance of Mental Growth in Infant and Child*	Macmillan, 1930
14.	Gesell, A. & Thompson, H.	*Learning and Growth in Identical Twins*	Gen. Psy. Monograph VI, 1929
15.	Gesell, A. Amatruda, C. Castner, B. Thompson, H.	*Biographies of Child Development*	Hamish Hamilton, 1939
16.	Goodenough, F.	*Measurement of Intelligence by Drawings*	World Book Co., 1926
17.	Griffiths, R.	*Imagination in Young Children*	Kegan Paul, 1935
18.	Isaacs, S.	*Intellectual Growth in Young Children*	Routledge, 1930
19.	Isaacs, S.	*Social Development in Young Children*	Routledge, 1933
20.	Jenkinson	*What Do Boys and Girls Read?*	Methuen
21.	Lewis, M. M.	*Infant Speech*	Kegan Paul, 1936

MODERN CHILD PSYCHOLOGY

22. Mead, M.	*An Investigation of the Thought of Primitive Children, with Special Reference to Animism*	J. Roy, Anth. Inst., LXII, 1932
23. Moore	*The Mental Development of the Child*	Psy. Review Mon. Supplement No. 3, 1906
24. Murphy, L. B.	*Social Behaviour and Child Personality*	Columbia Univ., 1937
25. Piaget, J.	*Language and Thought of the Child*	Kegan Paul, 1926
26. Piaget, J.	*Judgment and Reasoning in the Child*	Kegan Paul, 1928
27. Piaget, J.	*Child's Conception of the World*	Kegan Paul, 1929
28. Piaget, J.	*Child's Conception of Causality*	Kegan Paul, 1930
29. Piaget, J.	*The Moral Judgment of the Child*	Kegan Paul, 1932
30. Preyer	*The Senses and the Will*	New York, 1909
31. Scupin, E. & G.	{ *Bubis Erste Kindheit* { *The Early Childhood of the Boy*	Grieben, Leipzig, 1907
32. Shepherd, F.	*Responses of Infants in Feeding Situations and in the Period Antecedent to the Feeding Situation*	Unpub. Thesis., London, 1940
33. Shinn, M.	*Notes on the Development of a Child*	Vol. IV, 1907, Univ. Calif. Press
34. Shinn, M.	*Biography of a Baby*	Univ. Press, Berkeley, 1909
35. Shirley, M.	*The First Two Years* (3 Vols.)	Univ. Minn. Press, 1933
36. Stern, W.	*Psychology of Early Childhood*	Allen & Unwin, 1924
37. Stutsman, R.	*Mental Measurement of the Pre-School Child*	Harrap, 1931
38. Terman, L. & Merrill, M.	*Measuring Intelligence*	Harrap, 1937
39. Tiedeman, E.	*Observations on the Development of Mental Ability of the Child*	Trans. Murchison. Ped. Sem., 1927
40. Valentine, C. W.	*The Psychology of Early Childhood*	Methuen, 1942
41. Watson, J. B. & Watson, R. R.	*Studies in Infant Psychology*	Scientific Monthly. Vol. XIII, 1921

42. Society for Research in Child Development, National Research Council, Washington, 1936
Personality Development in Childhood
by Jones, M. C., and Burks, B. S.

43. Bowley, A. H.	*A Study of the Factors Influencing the General Development of the Child During the Pre-School Years, by Means of Record Forms*	Monograph Supplement XXV, B. J. Psy.

SECTION II

IN the following chapters I intend to give a summarized account of the normal development of children including some reference to the particular difficulties that may occur at different stages of growth. The facts given in these chapters are all based on either the knowledge obtained from research work, much of which has been reported in the previous section, or on my own personal experience of normal, subnormal and abnormal children from a wide variety of home backgrounds, of all ages, and of both sexes. The exact borderlines of normality are hard indeed to define, and there are few parents who will allow one to describe their children as just ordinary children. A school psychologist has perhaps rather an unique opportunity to study both the individual child and also children in the mass. In my experience I have never yet found two children really alike, and I should be hard put to it to describe the "average child" with any conviction. The norms given are based, of course, on carefully standardized tests, but individual variation is one of the most endearing characteristics of human nature.

CHAPTER I

BABYHOOD

I N the "bad" old days, mothercraft was not treated very scientifically. Babies were born, and often died, in quick succession. Little was known about scientific infant-feeding. Superstition was rife—what the mother saw or felt during pregnancy was thought to influence the unborn child for his future good or ill. The baby was swathed in many shawls and many petticoats, and closely protected from too much fresh air. Many old wives' tales were told of the dire consequences of different methods of treatment. Grandparents predicted the child's future career with authority. It is probable, however, that the baby was surrounded by loving care as well as much sentiment, and in modern days the scientific rearing of young children—which suggests the rearing of chicks in an incubator —may have lost much of the genuineness of maternal feeling and the spontaneity of expression. Our great grandparents, no doubt, sang and rocked their babies to sleep, spoon-fed them to a late age, and fondled and fussed over them unhesitatingly.

Many psychologists, nowadays, would prefer the great grandmother's methods in so far as they expressed natural affection and helped the baby to feel loved and wanted and secure, although his growing up may have been retarded and made somewhat more difficult by these methods.

I saw a boy of nine recently whose father had died when he was a few months old. His mother, anxious to keep the family business going, delegated the care of the baby to two nurses in a maternity home. She visited him at weekends, but never interfered with his upbringing because she thought they must know best. At the age of nine she had taken him to live with her, and was surprised to find that he took advantage of his new freedom to go off on adventures of his own, and took money to spend lavishly. She also learned for the first time that ever since he was a little boy he usually cried

52 MODERN CHILD PSYCHOLOGY

himself to sleep because he wanted his own mother. A little spoiling and a normal home life would have made all the difference to that boy.

Another baby I know had a particularly difficult upbringing. Her mother was a nervous, over-wrought and unstable woman. She became so difficult and unreliable at times that her baby had often to be taken from her and given to a neighbour to take care of. Later, the mother had to have treatment in a mental hospital. On her return, she was tragically drowned while trying to rescue her other child. At the outbreak of war Mary was ten years of age, and was evacuated to America, where she spent a very happy five years. On her return she found a stepmother and a baby stepbrother. It is no wonder that she found adjustment a little difficult, and that her parents were apprehensive lest she develop the same traits as her mother. Psychological investigation revealed a panic feeling that she might die—an acute fear of death and a perfectionist ideal of herself quite out of keeping with her true nature. Clearly, she had felt acutely frightened and insecure in babyhood.

The most essential part of the baby's upbringing is that he shall feel secure and happy as often as possible, and insecure and frightened as seldom as possible.

In the pre-natal condition, the foetus is kept warm, safe and comfortable in the mother's womb. Birth—the physical exertion, the sudden change of temperature, the loss of the ease and comfort of his position, the contact with hard surfaces, strange lights and noises, and the parting from his mother in a very literal sense—must involve a serious disturbance to his psychic equilibrium as well as to his physical condition.

He greets his new environment with a cry—if he is a healthy baby—and he sleeps as often as possible in the first few months, shutting out all the disturbing stimuli which impinge on his senses. His great craving, however, is for food and in his waking moments his mind and his body seem concentrated to gain this end. It is not, therefore, in the least surprising to find that the keenest intellectual activity and the strongest emotional expression are shown in relation to the feeding process. The baby adapts his body, watches for his mother, gazes at her

NORMAL DEVELOPMENT OF THE CHILD 53

face: he shows eagerness and delight when his need is satisfied, anxiety and anger when it is frustrated.

The healthy, comfortable baby, who is well fed and well cared for, appears placid and contented. The ailing baby, ill at ease, undernourished and carelessly looked after, appears unhappy and disturbed.

EMOTIONAL LIFE IN BABYHOOD

There is reason to think that the young baby has an active emotional life, and that his feelings are intense, fluctuating and often uncontrolled. The worst possible situation for him is to feel deserted, hungry, lonely and helpless. He is entirely dependent on the actions of grown-ups, and his fear of desertion and starvation must be a real and acute one. A child deprived in babyhood may feel deprived and insecure for much of his life.

Hospitalization in the early months can be very disturbing. Babies suffering from "wasting disease" or similar troubles, are frequently treated in hospital. Although his illness may be cured, and he may be well fed and cared for, his loss of personal affection may be very great. The result may be especially damaging in the second year if he has to be away for a considerable time with scarlet fever or diphtheria, or a series of infectious illnesses. His mother may peep at him through a screen, but she cannot reach him. He must feel desperately alone and abandoned with no assurance of return. Often such children will fret so consistently that the infectious trouble is superseded by quite severe anxiety states. I have known of babies who were given sedatives for sleeplessness, and cases of neurasthenia diagnosed in infancy. Whenever practicable, a young baby should be nursed at home, but better still, contact with a source of infection should be prevented in the early period. Good food, exercise, fresh air, sleep, adequate clothing are good preventatives.

It is clear then from a study of young babies and from psycho-analytic work that *fear* is a very acute feeling in babyhood, and it should be the mother's first concern to prevent it or allay it immediately. Probably waking at night in the dark in pain or in hunger is one of the worst experiences a

54 MODERN CHILD PSYCHOLOGY

baby can suffer unless his cries are heeded immediately and comfort and reassurance given him.

PSYCHOLOGICAL ASPECTS OF FEEDING

The feeding situation is all-important. Disturbed feeding, inadequate feeding or unsuitable feeding can have far-reaching physical and psychological results. Breast feeding at regular intervals, if the milk is satisfying and digestible, is obviously best for both the mother and the child. A baby who is well fed is less concerned with inner sensations and has more time and energy to show interest in the external world. He will look and listen; he will begin to reach and handle; he will seek to explore his immediate environment—his mother's breast, her body, her face, and her clothes, his own body and clothes, his cot and coverings. From these rudimentary beginnings, the foundations of perception and conception, of reasoning and thought, are laid.

What happens to the baby who is not properly fed? We know what happens to his body, but what about his mind? Naturally, we can only surmise and base our conclusions on scientific studies of the mind. It is obvious that an unsatisfied craving sets up acute feelings of frustration, of anger and of hate. These must be directed towards the mother, or person who fails to supply his need. To his mind, she must appear "bad." We have here the basis of the fairy tale theme of poisoning—the witch in *Snow White* who poisons with an apple is surely symbolic of the hateful and hating mother. We may go further and assume that the infant feels full of vengeful bad feelings directed towards his mother when he is frustrated. Outwardly they may be shown in tempers—even in biting and screaming—a form of "oral" attack on the mother. The desire to destroy must be strong also, and such feelings are followed by acute anxiety feelings. In later life, we have a counterpart in the child who cannot eat meat—is afraid to bite, and the adult who is a vegetarian—afraid of infantile "cannibalism." This may seem an extreme view, but it is sufficient to make clear the viewpoint that frustration in regard to feeding during infancy should be avoided at all costs. To my mind it is psychologically correct to give the baby a little

NORMAL DEVELOPMENT OF THE CHILD 55

food if he wakes in the night. It is interesting to note that, in the shelters during air raids, mothers instinctively suckled their babies when they cried, and this no doubt gave comfort to both mother and child.

On the other hand, to feed the baby every time he cries is most unwise. He should only be fed irregularly in an emergency. He must learn quite early to tolerate a little frustration, to wait for a little time, even though his needs seem urgent. The older he gets the more certain he is of his mother's ultimate willingness to satisfy him and so his ability to tolerate frustration is greater.

Weaning is liable to be a psychological disturbance to the infant. Naturally, if it is started early and done very gradually, the disturbance is decreased, but the loss of close contact with the mother, which bottle-feeding, and solid feeding implies, is a serious one. This constitutes the first step to independence, and usually the baby is most unwilling to take it. His fear of rejection and desertion may be intense. A mishandling of the situation by a sudden or abrupt weaning and subsequent supply of unsuitable foods is liable to cause future feeding troubles. Refusal to eat, food fads, indigestion and constipation, and kindred troubles may all be psychological in origin. Food becomes an emotional issue. It may represent "bad" objects to the child, and he may be afraid to eat. He knows too that such behaviour causes annoyance or anxiety to his mother, and he is thus assured of some emotional response. Nowadays, most mothers introduce new food and different tastes in the early months, and the baby accepts glucose, orange juice and cod-liver-oil quite happily. Working-class mothers vary greatly in their knowledge of dietetics. I know of one mother who suckles a child of eighteen months and another who gives her seven-month-old baby a potato chip with a half-empty bottle of "pop" to suck!

Toilet training is an allied subject to feeding. Here again the layman is liable to regard the psychologist's views as extravagant and far-fetched. Clinical work with adults and children suffering from neurotic troubles will convince the most severe critic, however, that emotional factors play their part in causing digestive troubles.

56 MODERN CHILD PSYCHOLOGY

The child may regard the contents of his body as "bad" and harmful. He may thus seek to withhold them for a long period—psychological constipation, or may refuse to void them in the accustomed place. He may also regard them as powerful and dangerous. He may then soil himself or his bed as an aggressive act—usually towards a hated stepmother or foster-mother.

The baby, of course, does not have sufficient muscular control or understanding to avoid wetting or soiling, but he will quickly appreciate that the whole matter is one of emotional concern to his mother. His accidents will be regarded with some disapproval and his successes will be smiled upon. Anxiety, annoyance or disgust—in fact, any marked feeling—expressed in relation to this matter will be quickly detected by the young infant and will serve to increase his disturbing phantasies about bad bodily contents.

The moral of this discussion, of course, is to treat the matter calmly and dispassionately. Toilet training should not be attempted too early, and relapses should not be unduly noticed. The child has done well if he has gained full bowel and bladder control by *two* years of age. Much incontinence after that age is indicative of emotional disturbance, and may or may not be related to early mistakes in training.

VOCALIZATION

The infant has well-developed lungs, and he knows how to use them from the first day. His cries are his only sure way of making contact with his environment and drawing attention to his needs. When, in taking a case history, one is informed that baby screamed constantly, that the parents seldom had a good night's rest, and that a doctor had finally to administer drugs, it is obvious that something is seriously amiss. The cause may be physical—the baby may be ailing or have a weak digestion. Usually the difficulty is psychological as well. Ill-health causes minor discomfort. This induces anxiety or emotional disturbance. Crying is an expression of acute discomfort, and is a form of attack directed towards the environment. The act of screaming can also be very painful to the child and increases his feeling of aggression.

NORMAL DEVELOPMENT OF THE CHILD 57

Vocalizing is very different from crying. As the baby discovers that he can make different sounds by using his tongue and throat and speech mechanism in different ways, he experiments with his new-found faculty and produces a great variety of sound. This usually produces a delighted response and much encouragement from adults, and he continues to try to win their approval. He also hears many different sounds around him, and as he grows older, he begins to imitate them. By twelve months he can produce a recognizable word or two, and clearly understands a good deal of what is said to him. Vowels and labials are easiest to say, and gutturals and diphthongs the most difficult. He needs much practice in the use of his speech organs before he can produce the required sounds at will, and it is not until the second year of his life that he seems prepared to spend time and energy on the business of learning to talk.

The baby seems to delight in noise—that is, in the noise he makes himself, banging spoons, throwing bricks, waving bells and knocking the fire-irons about. He is, however, disturbed by very loud noises, especially if they are unfamiliar, and if he is not reassured by his mother's presence. He responds better to quiet, gentle voices than to loud, sharp ones. He is usually responsive to music and rhythm. He will listen to a tune on the piano or the radio with great pleasure, and will even beat time. He enjoys movement and is attracted by anything that moves.

INTELLECTUAL LIFE IN BABYHOOD

The baby's early attempts at speech are one indication of a lively intellectual growth, but there are many other indications which a careful observer can notice.

The baby experiences sensation very keenly. He feels hot and cold, hard and soft, steady and unsteady, pleasant and painful sensations. He experiences inner sensations—those of digestion, defecation, and the like. He experiences outer sensations from contact with objects in his environment, and through sensations of sight, sound and smell. In the first year, one can almost see him comparing different sensations, connecting one attribute with another, and recognizing similarities

58 MODERN CHILD PSYCHOLOGY

—in fact, building up *percepts* and *concepts*. He learns that certain qualities belong to certain things. He seems to integrate his thought processes and make simple generalizations. All this is, of course, very rudimentary, but very soon he seems to connect the sound of cups and spoons with the feeding process, the sight of his coat with going out, the sound of water running with preparations for his bath. This is a type of associative thinking, implying memory and recognition and forethought.

Very soon, too, he shows a capacity to solve some of his own problems—how to get his spoon into his mouth, how to kick his bootee off his foot, how to push his rattle through the bars of his cot. Some of this activity is in the nature of trial and error, but he quickly learns to repeat the performance at will. Just as Kohler's chimpanzee learned how to use a stick to secure the fruit he wanted, so the human infant discovers how to pull, push and reach what he wants by his own efforts, and by the use of the "tools" around him.

When a baby sits stolidly in his cot, apparently unaware of the events in his environment, without attempting to explore or experiment, one may usually judge that something is wrong. He may be ill, or he may be generally retarded, and by six months most doctors can judge obvious signs of mental defect —both the physical and mental stigmata will be obvious in the case of a Mongol, a Cretin, or a Hydrocephalic.

PERCEPTUAL DEVELOPMENT

In the case of the normal infant, five months is an important stage of development. A marked growth of perception takes place about that time. The baby seems to appreciate that what he feels or tastes is the same as what he sees. He relates his sense experiences to one another. Thence, his reaching becomes more accurate and his understanding more acute. He uses his mouth a great deal to help him discover the nature of the objects around him. Obviously, it is a highly sensitive organ, and of great value to him at this stage. Gradually, as he grows older, he relies more on visual and tactual sensations, without reference to his mouth.

The baby begins to handle things with greater precision

NORMAL DEVELOPMENT OF THE CHILD 59

towards the end of the first year, and can reach with greater accuracy.

DEVELOPMENT OF MOVEMENT AND LOCOMOTION

To the watching parents the development of movement and locomotion within the first twelve months seems little short of a miracle. In the period of one year the baby grows from a helpless, wriggly, sleepy bundle of flesh and bones into a sturdy, upright, lively and rather independent youngster.

In the first few weeks purposive *positive* movements are almost entirely connected with feeding. The baby adapts his body for feeding, but very soon begins to make movements with his hands at the breast as well as with his lips. Later he will pat and fondle the breast and show interest in touching his mother's face and person. At *four months* he can seldom hold anything in his hand, but at *six months* old he can clutch at a dangling ring.

Negative defensive movements are more obvious in the first few weeks. The baby shrinks from a bright light, starts at a loud sound, and blinks or turns his head when some object is held too close to his face. As he becomes more accustomed to his environment, and is less easily disturbed or surprised, these defensive movements are not so frequent.

Spontaneous random movements, probably in response to some internal stimuli can be observed in the first month of life, but they are not very frequent when so much of the baby's time is spent in sleeping and eating. He does not as yet show much interest in exploring his surroundings. As a six-year-old remarked of his month-old baby brother: "he just eats and sleeps and cries," which seems a good summary of the young baby's repertoire. The astute observer will, however, note little curling movements of his fingers and wriggling movements of his toes in the bath or when waiting for a feed. It is from these small beginnings that the baby gradually explores the qualities of his universe. He learns that certain things are hot or cold, hard or soft, dry or wet, rough or smooth. We have noted that it is not until about five months of age that the infant seems to realize that what he sees is the same thing as what he feels—it looks white and it feels soft and fluffy, and it is

60 MODERN CHILD PSYCHOLOGY

always on his cot, i.e. his blanket. Before that age it seems that he experiences only numerous vague and disconnected sensations as he explores his immediate environment.

Another type of movement is known as *reflex activity*. This may be positive as in the case of suckling, swallowing, or grasping, or negative in the case of blinking, coughing, sneezing, and knee jerking. The infant is thus equipped at birth with certain forms of perfectly prepared behaviour to enable him to deal immediately with certain emergencies. Obviously without these he would not survive long, and these unlearned automatic actions subserve life directly.

As a healthy infant develops, the large muscles become stronger and he begins to show signs of definite movement of the whole body.

At one month old he can lift his head now and then.

This enables him to obtain a wider range of exploration, and he begins no doubt to feel less helpless and dependent when he can see people around him, and gains reassurance from familiar objects and persons within his view.

At two months old he can wave his legs and arms about when lying prone.
At three months old he can hold his head erect steadily.

At the same time, of course, his periods of wakefulness are longer, and he has more energy and time to explore his surroundings visually. He is usually most lively just before bath time at night, and most mothers take the trouble to play a little while with him then. Later as he gains in confidence he will enjoy water play in the bath—a valuable part of his general education.

At five months he can sit with slight support.
At six months he can sit alone for a short time.

At this age a very definite advance is noted. When the baby can sit in his cot or pram, he can observe his surroundings with far greater ease, and once again his sense of helplessness must be appreciably decreased. He can reach more easily for what he wants, and he can vocalize with greater energy and effect. He is definitely more a person, and commands more respect. He also scrutinizes faces more carefully, and recognizes

NORMAL DEVELOPMENT OF THE CHILD 61

strangers whom he usually regards with a hostile stare, and welcomes familiar faces with a smile.

At seven months most babies can roll over.

This is the beginning of locomotion. The baby can change his position and so make himself more comfortable, and sometimes get what he wants for himself. Most mothers are careful to let the child of this age have plenty of opportunity to kick and exercise his limbs on the floor or in the bath.

By nine months the baby has usually learned to crawl.

By this means he makes himself far more the master of his environment. Of course a great many children never crawl at all, but develop their own characteristic form of locomotion, propelling themselves along on their buttocks or rolling on their sides with consequent damage to their clothes. The form of locomotion chosen in these early days seems largely accidental—the baby hitting on some method which enables him to reach something he wants and then repeating this at will.

I think it is true to say that when a baby learns to get about on all fours, or by any other method, his anxieties are considerably reduced (though his mother's are increased!). He is able to know what his mother is doing, where she is, and to follow her about to some extent. He can go in and out of rooms and fetch what he wants and explore his environment for himself. He feels more powerful and more able to control himself and his environment to his liking.

At ten months he can pull himself to a standing position.

Provided that he is not discouraged, and is given sufficient opportunity, the child will pull himself up in his cot or in his play-pen, and will repeat this feat again and again obviously enjoying himself. He soon learns to stand alone, and so is able to reach for what he wants.

By thirteen months he can walk alone for a few steps.

And thus true locomotion is achieved, and the toddler is well and truly on his feet, and ready for every kind of adventure around the corner.

These milestones of development must not be taken too literally however. They represent the norms of motor development, and the average child will reach these stages of develop-

62 MODERN CHILD PSYCHOLOGY

ment at approximately these ages. But there are considerable individual differences. Some children are weakly and suffer frequent illnesses. Some are not given the opportunity for experiment and exploration. Some endure frequent changes of nurses or homes, or experience many disturbances in their early life. In all such cases development is likely to be slower or more erratic. Usually small setbacks are made up for by more rapid development later.

Although a child needs adequate stimulation and encouragement to achieve these skills, nature also plays her part. When the organism is ready and sufficiently mature the particular function will develop and the child be urged to walk or talk at the proper time given a normal environment and normal care.

CHAPTER II

THE CHILD IN THE NURSERY

BEFORE making a scientific study of the period from two to five years, it is worth considering the child as an individual.

Jeannie's parents were country folk. Her father was a farm labourer, her mother of Irish extraction. She was one of a large family with one younger sister and two older brothers. Jeannie was a determined young person, four years of age with fly-away hair and a mischievous smile. She had fallen in and out of the brook several times. She was always ready for adventure. She was in and out of neighbours' cottages, collecting a biscuit here and an apple there. She threw stones at the cats, ate unripe plums, bossed her younger sister about, went to bed very late, playing in the lamplight of the village street and making conversation with the visitors to the village pub. She seemed to have brought herself up, and had certainly developed a strong character by the age of four years. Her mother could be heard roaring at her from time to time, but Jeannie usually paid scant heed. I think she felt a little neglected. There seemed so many babies about, but in general, Jeannie was a favourite in the village, and won first prize as a black piccaninny in the local gymkhana. I think very probably Jeannie will be capable of tackling her problems in life as she meets them, and though she has had a rather haphazard upbringing, I doubt if she is much the worse.

Paul was a highly intelligent two-year-old whose father was a university professor. He was a serious, thoughtful youngster, bent on solving his own problems, but he had a wicked twinkle in his eye and was full of fun. He gave his elder sister of five a harassing time when she was in charge. He usually preferred his own company in the nursery class, and would be busy erecting an imposing edifice in the sand pit or clambering to the top of the jungle gym. Occasionally he would be captured by the older children to be a "horse"

64 MODERN CHILD PSYCHOLOGY

or a "passenger" or a "baby," but he usually managed to escape after a time. He had a most intelligent and enlightened upbringing, and was far in advance of his years intellectually. I think his future development is likely to be interesting.

Mickie, on the other hand, was definitely a son of the people. He lived in a sordid neighbourhood, in a wretched, overcrowded house with swarms of babies. His playground was the street and his toys often the residue of dust-bins. He was always chewing dirty bits of bread and marge. He seemed very deprived both materially and emotionally. He had been breast-fed very late and weaned suddenly. He had to tolerate the other babies being suckled. Apparently he was rather jealous of them. He was known to suck and chew anything he could get hold of, including his coat sleeve and bits of newspaper. He also wet his bed at night. On the other hand, at the age of five, he was a most engaging youngster, full of interesting ploys and constructive ideas, though he was not remarkable for his intelligence. Unless this boy's poverty of emotional experience can be made good, I think it is likely that he will become a delinquent as he grows older. His mother lacks intelligence and much knowledge of hygiene and housekeeping, and her standard of home-making leaves much to be desired from an economic and a maternal standpoint.

A little girl of two and a half years, adopted in infancy, had much ill-health, and rather neurotic and anxious adoptive parents to care for her. She was highly intelligent, but her emotional troubles were legion. I have seen her rushing about a large empty hall, following a children's Christmas party, shrieking with all her might in a kind of maniac way at the bogies she seemed to imagine in all the dark corners. I heard later how on one occasion at school, at the age of three, she ran screaming round the playground shouting at the children to stop their balls rolling in case they got lost (they had been told to be very careful with them), and then throwing herself on the grass, sobbing bitterly in a kind of anxiety attack. However, despite these turbulent times, she weathered the storms, and with psychological treatment and some parental guidance, she had developed into a happier and more placid child by the age of four.

NORMAL DEVELOPMENT OF THE CHILD 65

Such examples as these could be multiplied many times. This age is a fascinating one to study, but I do not think it is particularly easy or happy for the child. He learns a tremendous amount at this stage of growth, but it is often learning with tears.

GROSS MOTOR DEVELOPMENT

Perhaps the most evident and most delightful development to watch is the child's gradual mastery over his limbs, and his growth in muscular control. At two years old he is only a toddler, often unsteady on his feet. He rapidly gains in confidence, and by three years he is *walking* and *running* with ease. From then on he strives to perform many physical feats. He learns to balance, to climb, to jump, to skip and to hop. He will practise these achievements over and over again, and if you give him nothing from which to jump and nothing on which to climb, your drawing-room furniture and your garden gate will suffer. Any type of strong wheel toy—a wheel-barrow, a trolley, a Kiddie-Kar, a tricycle—will help him to gain mastery over these skills and provide him with much agreeable exercise.

Of course the child may be handicapped by a poor physique or he may be unusually timid, this latter attitude being often induced by an over-protective attitude on the part of his parents. He needs encouragement to be adventuresome and a little daring. The neurotic child is often fearful of experimenting and unwilling to join in rough-and-tumble games.

Movement to music, rhythmic activity, is often beneficial to children of this age. They gain greater control as well as greater grace and facility in movement. Eurythmics in some form or other are much enjoyed by the four-year-old.

FINE MOTOR CO-ORDINATION

Control of smaller muscles comes later than the control of the larger muscles. During the pre-school years, the child needs large-scale material in the way of blackboards and chalks, large sheets of paper and large paint brushes. He needs opportunity for large-scale movement until he has learned better eye

E

66 MODERN CHILD PSYCHOLOGY

and hand co-ordination. No child should be taught to write until he is at least five years of age.

He will enjoy all sorts of manipulative activities during this period—threading beads, large-scale weaving, fitting toys, and handling many different. materials. In the nursery school he will learn to hang up his own coat, do up his own shoes, wash his own mug, sweep up the sand when he spills it, cut paper and model with clay or plasticine. If he is given opportunity he will find real zest in doing these simple things for himself, and will usually resent adult interference.

VISUAL PERCEPTION

The child's perception of size, shape, colour and volume gradually becomes more accurate, and he enjoys any activity which gives him an opportunity to practise his new skills in the perceptual field. Matching colours or shapes, sorting out different sizes and shapes, doing simple jig-saws—any type of sense-training apparatus will be an attraction to a child of this age. Most children cannot name colours correctly until about *five years of age*, but they can match them, and distinguish differences long before—at least by three years of age.

Time sense is poorly developed as yet. The child has insufficient experience to judge this correctly. He lives so much in the present, and seems to show scant interest in the past or the future. It is therefore most important to avoid confusing the child or making rash promises. "I shall be back soon" may seem hours of time to the child left alone. "We'll go there another day" may seem almost never to the child anticipating pleasure. "I'll get it for you to-morrow" means keen disappointment. "We'll have dinner in a few minutes" usually conveys little definite idea of the time to wait for a young child. Of course, he learns quickly enough, but it is most unwise to tell a child of an exciting event a long way ahead— a birthday party, or the arrival of a favourite relation should be announced not weeks ahead, but a few days only.

THE DEVELOPMENT OF SPEECH

In the preceding chapter we have seen that the rudiments of speech are apparent in the first year of life. *Crying* and

NORMAL DEVELOPMENT OF THE CHILD   67

screaming are characteristic of the very young infant, but differentiations in intensity and quality can be detected after the first month. Crying at first indicates a state of discomfort and unsatisfied needs. *Babbling* on the other hand occurs later and indicates a state of comfort and contentment. Vocal sounds, such as "ah" and "eh", are usually the first to be heard. The labials, b, p, m, generally come next, probably because the labial muscles used in their production have already been well exercised in sucking at the breast or bottle. Guttural sounds, g, k, tend to follow. The sibilants, s, sh, z, and the liquid sounds, r, and l, are usually the last to be sounded, depending as they do on greater control and mobility of the tongue, or on dentition.

This babbling and crowing stage seems to be a type of vocal play, the baby evidently gaining great pleasure from endless repetitions of sounds, such as mamama and nanana. The tongue becomes active by three months of age, and by six months of age most vowel and consonant sounds can be detected in the infant's babbling monologue, or *lalling* as it is termed. The more appreciation and approval he receives, the more he will continue to try out new sounds and begin to show interest in imitating the speech sounds of adults.

Usually by *ten months* of age the child succeeds in using *one word* significantly. By *twelve months* of age the average child has a vocabulary of *three or four* distinguishable words.

But great individual differences are noted by all careful observers depending on intelligence, health, encouragement, opportunity and environmental influences. I recently saw a boy of three years who had a vocabulary of 100 words at twelve months of age, but certainly by three years he had a bad stammer!

A good cultural environment, a good pattern of adult speech, and normal encouragement facilitates language development. High intelligence is correlated with early speech development. Feeble-minded children may not start to talk until nearly three years of age, and their vocabulary and mastery of language forms grows very slowly. Excellent health and great physical activity may be conducive to slowness in speech development because the child tends to devote more of his

68   MODERN CHILD PSYCHOLOGY

time and energy to learning to walk and to acquiring other physical skills. Girls tend to talk earlier and their vocabulary develops more rapidly than that of boys. They tend to maintain their advantage through all stages of linguistic development.

After the first word has been spoken the child's vocabulary grows very slowly, one or two words being made to act as maids of all work, assuming a different meaning according to the context. After eighteen months, however, it begins to increase rapidly. The following norms were obtained by Smith[1] from carefully standardized vocabulary tests:

Age	No. of Cases	Vocabulary	Terman's Results Age	Vocabulary
1·0	52	3	8 yrs.	3,600
1·6	14	22	10 yrs.	5,400
2·0	25	272	12 yrs.	7,200
2·6	14	446	14 yrs.	9,000
3·0	20	896	Average Adult	11,700
3·6	26	1,222	Superior Adult	13,500
4·0	26	1,540		
4·6	32	1,870		
5·0	20	2,072		
5·6	27	2,289		
6·0	9	2,562		

It is interesting to compare these figures with those obtained by Terman from a test list of 100 words selected to represent adequately and fairly the contents of the ordinary dictionary. He obtained his figures by determining the standards for different years by the vocabulary reached by 60 to 65 per cent of the subjects at the various mental levels.

At first the child's attempts at verbal expression and communication are "sentence words," or "one-word sentences." "Up" means "Put me up there now." "Mama" may mean "Mother come here quickly." "No" means "Take it away at once. I don't like it." This economical form of language, usually accompanied by gesture and facial expression, can be surprisingly effective, and may satisfy the child for many months.

[1]Smith, M. E. *The Development of the Sentence and Extent of Vocabulary in Young Children*. University of Iowa, 1926.

NORMAL DEVELOPMENT OF THE CHILD   69

By two and a half years a slightly more complex type of sentence may be expected, but children vary tremendously in this respect. I know one little girl of *twenty-two months* who remarked clearly and precisely on seeing the new moon, which had changed from white to yellow as the darkness fell, "Look! The moon's got a light in it."

The following norms obtained by Smith from a study of 124 children show how the sentence gradually increases in size and complexity.

DEVELOPMENT OF THE SENTENCE FROM TWO TO FIVE YEARS (SMITH)

Age	No. of Cases	Words per sentence (average)
2·0	11	1·7
2·6	18	2·4
3·0	17	3·3
3·6	23	4·0
4·0	17	4·3
4·6	22	4·7
5·0	16	4·6

In general it is found that after *interjections*, nouns and verbs are the most popular parts of speech for the young child. At first he may refer to himself by name, "John do it," but gradually personal pronouns appear at about the end of the second year. "John do it" becomes "Me do it," and then "Let me do it," or "I can do it." Adverbs, then adjectives soon begin to appear more frequently, and conjunctions, prepositions and relational elements tend to appear last.

Language, therefore, tends to grow from the simpler forms to the more complicated, and from crude and confused expression to the subtle and more defined.

Children who are brought up in institutions tend to talk later and to have a more limited vocabulary than children brought up in a more favourable environment who receive more individual attention. Children learn readily from each other except twins, who are generally slow in language development, probably because they learn to understand each other

70 MODERN CHILD PSYCHOLOGY

so quickly by means of gesture, tone and a few words, usually unintelligible to adults. Stimulation from adults, and a high cultural level of home background are conducive to good speech development. Very intelligent children, who use abstract concepts probably more than practical concepts, tend to employ words a great deal, and acquire new ones rapidly.

Over-pressure, or the reverse, lack of encouragement, are both harmful to good speech development. The former often induces a stammer, and the latter slows up language development. A limited environment with little opportunity for new experiences prevents rapid acquirement of new words. Persistence of baby talk is usually due to excessive attention being paid to it by adults, or the child may find it the best way of ensuring his mother's interest. As soon as a child is able to pronounce words correctly he should be encouraged to do so.

The pre-school period from two to five years has been called the golden age of language. Interest in learning to speak, in acquiring new words, and delight in asking questions are commonly found.

SOCIAL-EMOTIONAL DEVELOPMENT

It is fitting that these two aspects of development should be discussed together because one influences the other to a great extent.

The first important emotional relationship of a child is that towards his parents. Until he has achieved a happy, easy, natural relationship toward them, his efforts at social co-operation are not likely to be very successful. If he is unsure of his parents' affection, insecure and afraid, he does not readily make advances to other people. If he is over-possessed by his parents, and very dependent on them, he will not seek emotional response beyond the family circle. If he is very antagonistic towards them, he tends to greet the rest of the world of grown-ups with hostility. Once he is sure of his parents' love and friendliness, of which normally by this age he should have had full experience, he will expect friendliness from outsiders and will welcome social advances. Many babies of twelve and

NORMAL DEVELOPMENT OF THE CHILD 71

eighteen months will do so; with others, such development is not much in evidence until two or three years.

Again his emotional relationship to his brothers and sisters is all important. Some degree of jealousy and rivalry is to be expected, but normally this is tempered by loyalty, friendliness and pleasure in each other's companionship. Moreover the younger generation will support each other against the tyranny of adults, and often present a solid and defiant front against their demands. This is a healthy sign of emotional development representing the child's normal rebelliousness and independence, and indicates that he is not too greatly under the influence of the dangerous, controlling parental figures which he has built up in his unconscious mind.

But when jealousy and rivalry are intense, when competition for maternal love is very keen, it is natural that other children will at first be regarded as rival claimants for the attention of any loved adult. Hostility and hate is the natural response to any rival, and a child greatly disturbed by such family conflicts cannot make friendly advances at first.

Thus one may expect turbulent feelings and strong expression of them in speech, play or behaviour. All careful observers note the prevalence of aggressive play and speech in the preschool period, and it is essential for good emotional and social development that aggression finds a safe outlet at this time. Elsewhere I have quoted examples showing open aggressiveness in three- and four-year-olds from my own observation of young children. Isaacs and Murphy provide a great deal of evidence in their records of children. Strong aggressiveness has been found to be correlated with marked sympathetic feelings and points to what has been described as a "general outgoing tendency." This characteristic is indicative of a healthy emotional life. The child who restrains his feelings unduly, driving them underground, uses up a great deal of mental energy to prevent their reappearance into consciousness.

Naturally some repression, some control is necessary, and acts as a civilizing influence on the turbulent emotions of the young child. Parents and teachers encourage some degree of control over temper, destructiveness and aggression. But we know from intensive studies of young children that the child

72 MODERN CHILD PSYCHOLOGY

sets up a controlling influence within his own mind very early indeed, based on his early experience of frustration, and patterned on his parents' prohibitions to some extent. Elsewhere I have attempted to define satisfactory emotional development as implying some degree of serenity, contentment, normal demonstrativeness, courage, independence and alertness. Such a development is not usually apparent until well towards the end of this period—five years of age, and a young child's emotional behaviour will vary from day to day, even from hour to hour. Children from happy homes, possessing a good relationship to their parents, will build up satisfactory relationships outside the family far more quickly than in the reverse case.

The child's feelings of love and hate towards his parents and his conflicts in relation to them are described in the section on psycho-analytic findings, but the usual pattern is the boy's devotion to his mother and antagonism to his father, and the girl's devotion to the father and hostility towards the mother. These conflicts appear to be very intense between two and four years, but gradually subside and become less insistent and more controlled and diffused after that time. Experience of other children, the gradual widening of the family circle helps immeasurably.

The stages of social development, although by no means clear cut nor definite, have been described as follows:

To Adults
1. Dependence, eighteen months to *c.* two years.
2. Independence, defiance, two to three years.
3. Co-operation, three to four years.

To Children
1. Aloofness, *c.* two years.
2. Aggressiveness, *c.* three years.
3. Friendliness, *c.* four years.

RELATIONSHIP TO ADULTS

The toddler is still very dependent on his mother and on grown-ups generally. He is still a little unsteady on his feet, and rather limited in his speech, and there are still many things

NORMAL DEVELOPMENT OF THE CHILD 73

that he cannot do for himself. It is noticeable also that when another baby arrives, often when the older child is about two years old, that the first child becomes for a time very dependent on his mother. Parents have told me that they notice a distinct change in expression in photographs taken before the birth of the new baby and after. The child becomes more thoughtful, more anxious and less placid, often for a short time. Obviously the arrival of the new baby involves a difficult readjustment for the older child, one which involves time and thought, and he is clearly concerned lest he lose his mother's affection and close attention. After weaning, this is probably the most difficult crisis the child has to meet, and is in a way a second weaning. The situation needs to be handled with great tact, and the child needs every assurance of his mother's continuing love and care.

Defiance and independence denotes a healthy stage of emotional growth, and the ætiology of the temper tantrum which occurs rather frequently at this time is discussed later in these pages. Here again wise and considerate handling is necessary if this type of behaviour is not to persist beyond the baby stage, and parents should recognize that this bid for independence and rebellion against adult domination is a normal stage of growing up.

Co-operation and friendliness, of course, occurs at all stages of social growth, but usually it is not until after three years of age that they become the child's habitual response to adults. It seems as if the child must experiment first and prove that adults are kind, loving and reassuring before he feels safe to love them without fear of repulse or loss.

RELATIONSHIP TO CHILDREN

Provided the child's relations to adults proceed satisfactorily his relationship with children will also develop along sound lines. Naturally he at first will regard them with some suspicion or even disregard them altogether, intent on his own schemes and pursuits. Two-year-olds seldom play actively together, though they may like to play beside each other, and occasionally make contact. That is why in my opinion large nurseries for the toddler age are not satisfactory except in a war emergency.

74 MODERN CHILD PSYCHOLOGY

The very young child needs a close personal relationship with one adult, and that is not easy to arrange in a class of thirty two-year-olds. He may be disturbed by the number of children and the very clamour and urgency of their desires compete with his. He will be far happier in a small group of mixed ages, where the three- and four-year-old will naturally adopt the big brother or big sister rôle, and help him to deal with difficulties.

Three years of age is a much better time to begin nursery school education. He will then be ready for new activities and begin to enjoy companionship. He now takes his first lessons in learning social adjustment outside the family. He learns to fight his own battles; he learns to win and also to lose; he learns to lead and to follow. He discovers that his rivals can also be good companions, that it is safe to express antagonism and also affection openly, and that retaliation is not so terrifying nor so violent as he fears in his unconscious mind. Very often the child with whom he quarrels most is his best friend.

Despite the nuisance value to adults, this period of learning social adjustment is of immense value to the child. By four years of age the nursery is less like a battlefield resounding with the yells and storms of battle, with heated arguments concerning *meum* and *tuum*, with hair pulling and face slapping. Children lose their earnest possessiveness to some extent, probably because they are less apprehensive of loss of the real things that matter, their parents' love. They are more ready to settle their differences by compromise, and a gentleman's agreement, rather than a pitched battle, may be the outcome. Friendliness and co-operation to achieve a common aim are more noticeable. Unity against adults is a force that binds different temperaments together, and joint hostility is frequently noted at this age. This again is a healthy sign. It is a relief for a child to have allies, and discover that his fellows feel defiant and antagonistic towards grown-ups sometimes, too. Children also enjoy playing together in small groups, seldom more than three or four, in the sand pit, on the jungle gym., with dolls or trains. Dramatic and imaginative play takes on a new character, and the child's play is enriched while his social, emotional, and intellectual development proceeds apace.

NORMAL DEVELOPMENT OF THE CHILD 75

The emotional difficulties common to this period are discussed at the end of this section. Difficulties are likely to occur when so great a measure of social-emotional growth is achieved in so short a time.

INTELLECTUAL GROWTH

As his social and emotional growth proceeds, he is less concerned with personal problems, and can turn his interest outwards to the external world. Intellectual development can then proceed at a greater rate and by five years old there is more evidence of logical thought and abstract reasoning, and his thinking becomes less sense-tied, concrete or animistic. He still learns by doing, and the logic of action is more important to him than the logic of thought. Manipulative problems interest him, and he is eminently curious about the world around. His questions are an indication of this, and his language development is, of course, rapid. From then on it is a short step to interest in learning and school subjects. It is never wise to press this, and the child will show only too clearly when he is ready for formal work. Until then he needs opportunity for experiment and discovery mainly in a practical sphere, and the most reliable tests of intelligence are in the nature of performance tests at this age.

Of course, children vary both in their degree of innate intelligence and in their rate of development. The duller child plays longer and talks slower and thinks less quickly. The brighter child usually shows advanced speech development, learns more quickly from his mistakes, and, of course, appears more alert and interested in everything around him than his less fortunate companion. It is most important to gauge the mental age of the child and to judge his maturation rate before class placement is decided upon. Admittedly, intelligence is affected by three important factors. A poor physique or any specific physical defect may handicap his mental development. A limited environment, providing little stimulus or encouragement—such as an institution—may retard development. Also emotional inhibition, when the child is suffering from undue strain or excessive conflict, will prevent him doing justice to himself and his effective intelligence will appear much less

76 MODERN CHILD PSYCHOLOGY

than it really is. All these factors must be taken into account before any definite judgment is made about the child's general intelligence. Intelligence tests tend to be more reliable after seven years of age than before seven, because emotional factors influence his intellectual output more strongly at the earlier age.

THE PROBLEMS OF THE PRE-SCHOOL PERIOD

Certain difficulties between two and five years of age are so common as to be recognized as normal to this stage of growing up. It is important that those in charge of little children, in homes, nurseries or schools should appreciate the difficulties the child experiences in his emotional life and make allowance for him. It is outside the scope of this work to set out general suggestions for wise treatment of the child. This has been done elsewhere. It is obvious, however, that if the home environment lacks the essentials of good living, i.e. sufficient stability and security, warmth of affection and adequate freedom, tempered by proper discipline, the child will have greater difficulties than if his emotional needs are sufficiently met in his home.

TEMPER TANTRUMS

These are characteristic of the two-year-old who is learning independence and is testing out his parents. He needs assurance that they can help him to control his intense angry feelings when they boil over, as it were, and he will suffer immeasurably if he does not meet with wise restraint to temper his violence. Gradually, as he proves to himself that his tempers do not bring down irretrievable retribution, and that he can still rely on his parents' love despite his naughtiness, tantrums become less frequent. By the age of four they should not occur very often.

DESTRUCTIVENESS

This is often a form of experimentation. The child seeks to learn the how and why of things, and, of course, the kitchen clock or the wireless will suffer. Sometimes it is to show his own power, sometimes a form of sublimation. He destroys what he hates in an indirect or symbolic way. In clinical work,

NORMAL DEVELOPMENT OF THE CHILD 77

when the child is provided with suitable material and encouraged to express himself freely, the young child will bury, cut up, drown with water or hammer to bits little figures which represent the hated mother or father of his *un*conscious mind. In this way he gains relief and comes to terms with his emotion.

QUARRELSOMENESS

Quarrelsomeness, of course, is to be expected at these times when the child is learning the difficult art of social adjustment. He has to learn to take turns when his sense of possession and insistence on his own rights are very strong. If his rivalry with his brothers and sisters is very keen, his difficulties will be more apparent. The clash of opinion and purpose is bound to occur, but gradually he learns to compromise and also combine with others. It is far more healthy from a psychological point of view to be sometimes quarrelsome, pugnacious and determined than always docile, submissive and yielding. At three years of age quarrels are usually at their height, but between four and five years, children show real ability to play happily together for longer periods. After that time arguments and wordy battles tend to take the place of fisticuffs.

COMFORT HABITS, e.g. THUMB-SUCKING, MASTURBATION

These habits, which are rather common now, are generally a child's means of seeking comfort. Thumb-sucking is often a legacy from babyhood, and the child will return to a habit, which is a substitute for breast feeding, when he is frightened, anxious, lonely or bored.

Masturbation is another way of gaining pleasure and comfort, and occurs in much the same circumstances. From his bodily experimentation he discovers this method of gaining self-pleasure, and if the external world is too exacting or disturbing, he will seek satisfaction from such a bodily pleasure. As he comes to terms with his environment and learns to accept it, the habit will usually disappear.

FEARS AND ANXIETIES

Fears and anxieties in some form or another must be expected now and again at this time. Nightmares are fairly

78 MODERN CHILD PSYCHOLOGY

common and probably reflect the disturbance which is going on in the child's unconscious mind. Usually the terrifying figures of his dreams represent the parents in the guise of revengeful or retributive figures. His own wishes to destroy and damage are let loose, and he is terrified by the strength of his own feelings. Here emotional development and control, coupled with experience of real, kind and loving parents, will gradually reduce the persistence of nightmares.

Irrational fears, experienced in the daytime, are probably related to the same unconscious phenomenon, but in this case the fear is projected on to some animal or object in the external world which it is safe to hate and fear, and against which he can enlist protection and sympathy from his parents, e.g. dogs, cats, mice, or spiders.

The child who is persistently timid and nervous is not a normal child, and if acute fears and sleep disturbances are present, psychological treatment may be advisable.

In general, normal maturation and a normal environment will be sufficient to counteract most of these emotional difficulties, and by five years of age the child will appear much more stable and placid.

This state of mental health will be attained with much greater facility if he is allowed sufficient outlet in free play. His play during these years does not only provide an intellectual and social education, but also a valuable emotional outlet. His need to play out his inner thoughts and feelings is most pressing, and he needs space and scope and companions for this purpose. His media may be sand and water, clay or plasticine, bricks, paint or crayons, or dolls or teddy bears. He may dramatize all the familiar homely scenes which he witnesses every day—bathing and bedding and feeding and loving and hating—and by this means, he masters his own anxieties in relation to his own parents. Much has been written on this subject in recent years, and the value of free play to the preschool child is widely recognized nowadays.

PLAY

The psychology of play is a particularly fascinating subject and a good deal has been written about it. It has certainly

NORMAL DEVELOPMENT OF THE CHILD

assumed greater importance in the minds of educators, youth leaders, social workers, administrators as well as psychologists.

Herbert Spencer was one of the earliest psychologists to discuss play, and he defined it as *excess of energy* which the young person has in abundance and needs an outlet through play to discharge.

Karl Groos held that play should best be considered as a *preparation for life,* for the child learns through different play activities those mental and manual operations which he will need in later life. Just as a kitten plays with a cotton-reel as if it were a mouse, so the little child will play "house" or "school" and seek to imitate the behaviour of grown-ups.

Stanley Hall postulated the *Recapitulatory Theory* of play. He states that a child re-lives the life of his ancestors in his play, and plays hunting and fighting and home-making games which represent the way the primitive peoples live.

Montessori and *Froebel* stressed the educational value of play. Montessori devised a set of sense-training apparatus which are known and used widely. They are designed to help a little child to learn in a pleasurable way to distinguish between shapes, sizes, colours, height, weight, volume and sound. Although many modifications have been made and few teachers, except those teaching in a Montessori school, use the material exactly as it was originally designed, much modern sense-training apparatus owes its origin to the genius of Maria Montessori. Froebel has devised a most useful play method of teaching, or rather of introducing formal work gradually through the medium of play, and has designed some delightful play material. The Froebel approach to education is considered to be very sound, and a Froebel-trained teacher is recognized as a valuable and capable teacher.

Modern psychology stresses the social and emotional value of play. Through free play unorganized by adults, the young child learns to adapt to his playmates, to accept leadership, to make compromises, to co-operate in a common purpose, to defend property rights and to withstand antagonism. Through early play activities the child learns to abandon the egocentric position to some extent and to reciprocate and co-operate with other children. The simplest form of play is

80 MODERN CHILD PSYCHOLOGY

free muscular play—the rough and tumble, running, jumping, climbing, pulling, scrambling activities of the healthy young person. Such play is often enjoyed alone, and does not involve such close contact with other children. *Manipulatory play* is also primarily with things rather than with people—when the child explores and experiments with whatever material is available. *Destructive* and *constructive* play also involves the use of materials, but often three-year-old and four-year-old children will join together in some constructional activity with sand or clay or bricks and the pleasure of joint activity is first appreciated. But the older child spends more time in *dramatic* and *imitative play*. This involves the selection of rôles— mother, father and baby, engine-driver and passenger, horse and driver. A more difficult adjustment has to be made and much give and take is required.

In dramatic play the child gains too a valuable emotional outlet. By playing out family scenes the child gains release from emotional conflicts which surround his relationships to his parents and brothers and sisters. Lowenfeld[1] has written at length on this aspect of play, and has developed a therapeutic technique known as *projection therapy*, or *play therapy*.

PLAY THERAPY

This form of treatment is used widely in Child Guidance Clinics[2] nowadays. It is a method of giving the child opportunity to express himself freely in some form of play activity with whatever type of play material suits his purpose best. Just as verbalizing, talking about a terrifying experience brings relief to an adult, so a child needs to play out his feelings, and by dramatizing his inner fears and anxieties he learns to come to terms with them and to master them to some extent.

The very disturbed child may at first play in a very stilted or stereotyped way, and may seem afraid of expressing himself freely. Gradually as he gains confidence in his environment and in the play therapist, he tends to return to very infantile play and enjoys very messy games with sand and water. By

[1]Lowenfeld M. *Play in Childhood*. Gollancz, 1935.
[2]Ref.: Hawkey, M. L. *Play Analysis: Case study of a nine-year-old girl*, Vol. XX, Pt. III, 1945, pp. 236-43. Brit. I. Med. Psy.

NORMAL DEVELOPMENT OF THE CHILD 81

this means he expresses aggression in a very primitive form. Later he may paint or model or use miniature toys to represent the people in his world. He will project his feelings on to these toys, and often the nature of his conflicts can be more fully understood. It is then possible sometimes to explain in very simple terms what is worrying him—that he feels very jealous of his sister, or very antagonistic to his father. The mere fact of the acknowledgment of these feelings about which the child feels so guilty brings relief to him, and the understanding and sympathetic response he gains from the adult instead of reproof and condemnation helps him immeasurably. He realizes that it is perfectly natural to experience these emotions, and that in time he will learn to modify and control and re-direct them.

Gradually the character of his play changes, and though he may still need adequate outlet for aggression in some play form, this tendency will be less exaggerated, and he will be more capable of constructive and creative play. He will also be able to play more happily with other children, and can tolerate some frustration and rivalry more easily. Children are normally aggressive in some degree, and there are many play activities which permit them to express antagonism in a socially acceptable way—pillow fights, cowboys, skittles, football, and such occupations as hammering, sawing, cutting or modelling. Aggression only becomes dangerous when it is unduly repressed; it may then find an outlet in delinquency or some anti-social act. Play thus provides a valuable safety valve to the child.

F

CHAPTER III

THE CHILD IN THE SCHOOL

J O H N is a six-year-old—lively, talkative, and merry. He is the oldest of a family of four, and he is fully conscious of the importance of his position. His younger brother, Bill, is a devoted disciple, but his young sister, aged two, is markedly non-co-operative and frequently disturbs the peace of the home. John feels superior to family squabbles and to all "this baby business"—his youngest brother is one month old. His only apparent interest in the youngest is the prestige value he bestows on the household. As he remarked, "*We've* got a new baby now. When he is a bit older he can join our gang."

John has many and varied interests. He can spend happy hours on the nursery floor playing soldiers with his brother and "the gang." He can be busily and profitably employed writing and illustrating his first original story in a style and a spelling all his own. He will also amuse his young brother in bed at night by telling stories about an amazing and mythical character who has weird and wonderful adventures. He delights in doing sums in his head, insists that he can do £ s. d. now and divide by seven when the sweet ration has to be made to last out the week. When he went to London recently he concentrated his time and energy on trips to the Zoo (two in a week) and constant journeys up and down the moving staircases in the Underground (several times a day).

John is, in fact, an intelligent, normal six-year-old whose intellectual social and emotional development shows good promise.

Jennifer, aged eight (I.Q. 103), was a delightful little girl with long pigtails. She was described as happy-go-lucky and easy-going. She was an only child, but had lots of friends.

Her father worked on the railway and her mother did part-time work. Both parents were fond of Jennifer and had a

NORMAL DEVELOPMENT OF THE CHILD 83

good understanding of a child's needs, though perhaps they tended to be a little indulgent. They lived in a comfortable, clean, well-kept house in one of the better type of housing estates.

Jennifer loved school, was normally naughty, and a great reader. She still liked to play with dolls, enjoyed dancing, was a member of the Brownies, and went to the cinema whenever her mother would let her. She told me that if she had three wishes which would come true, she would like to be a fairy, wear pretty clothes and do magic, "turning people into nice things." She had a great love of neatness and order, and pretty things. She was a very healthy little girl and always ate and slept well. She did occasionally wet the bed, have "horrid dreams about ghosts," and bite her nails. With encouragement and help all the symptoms cleared up.

These and many others could be quoted. They come from just ordinary homes with sensible parents. Their charm lies in their liveliness, their versatility, their insatiable curiosity, their absorption in the interest of the moment, their concern with the common or garden things of life, their delight in practising new skills, and their healthy disregard for damaged knees and torn trousers.

I once asked a ten-year-old and his parents to tea. While the grown-ups admired the flowers and discussed the relative merits of fertilizers, the small boy examined the garden wall. In a minute we were hailed with the cry, "Hi, Dad, give us a match box. There are some swell chrysalis here, one's a Red Admiral, I think." And the rough old garden wall, uninteresting to grown-ups, provided him unending delight for the rest of the visit.

I took an eight-year-old boy to a new hostel. The warden suggested that he go and explore the garden. After about fifteen minutes I went to see how he was getting on. I found him in the middle of a group of grimy small boys round a bonfire, busily melting old lead piping in tin cans and pouring this into a "mould" of a pistol shaped in sand in an old biscuit tin! Each one eagerly waited his turn, and all helped to collect wood for the fire. A lively conversation was going on and an occasional smoke-filled eye or burnt finger was ignored. The

84 MODERN CHILD PSYCHOLOGY

next time I visited the hostel, bows and arrows were all the rage.

I asked a boy of eleven, who had a local reputation for delinquency, how he had spent his half-term holiday. "Coo, Miss, I had a whale of a time! My pal and I made a den in the woods. We borrowed a pick-axe and made a deep pit and boarded it over. Then we fortified it and defended it from the enemy. Mum gave us some eats and we spent all day up there."

INTERESTS

Children between the ages of five and eleven years show a great variety of interests. Collecting things, amassing all sorts of property, is one popular pursuit. Analyses of small boy's pockets have been made with illuminating results, showing a vast quantity of all sorts of odds and ends detrimental to the shape of the pocket. Children of this age will collect almost anything—conkers, marbles, shells, acorns, putty, coloured silks, pencils, tram tickets, cigarette cards, postcards, books, butterflies, wild flowers, train numbers and so on. This seems partly due to genuine interest which may later develop into a lifelong hobby, and partly to the sheer joy of possession with its accompanying feeling of power.

Boys and girls tend to show different interests and enjoy different play activities during these years.

Boys enjoy especially: games of speed and skill; all types of constructional activity, e.g. meccano, woodwork, making "dens," etc.; climbing and similar feats of athletic skill; country pursuits—keeping animals, cycling, camping, etc.; amateur engineering and scientific activities.

Their games tend to be more boisterous and energetic than girls' and this may be one reason why each sex prefers its own company usually. Girls tend to enjoy rather less active games and such pursuits as: family and school play; dressing up; decorating and simple handicrafts; simple needlecraft and knitting; games of chance and skill, e.g. ball games, skipping, ludo, etc.

The popularity of doll play usually dwindles after seven

NORMAL DEVELOPMENT OF THE CHILD   85

or eight years of age, and more elaborate "family" games take its place.

Girls of this age, just as boys, can be very "clannish," and may refuse to have anything to do with boys, or even with girls in a different class or different street. "Only" children often have imaginary companions. These seem to be compensatory in type and often represent everything that they would like to be themselves—pretty, clever, adventuresome, or naughty.

Both boys and girls may enjoy writing stories or poems, making maps or plans, drawing and painting of all types, and, of course, reading. When the child first learns to read—usually about six years of age, a new world opens up to him. I have seen four-year-olds even pretending to be like daddy and read the newspaper (upside down!). It is a grown-up kind of thing to do and hence assumes enhanced importance in their eyes. Intelligent children will often teach themselves to read long before they are six. They may even become thoroughly aggravating to their parents when they insist on spelling out advertisements, road signs, or bus stations at every opportunity. They can be equally tiresome when their noses are always in books. If they are really keen and normally intelligent, they will devour almost everything that comes their way—comics, newspapers, cheap magazines, annuals, fairy tales, animal stories, funny stories, school stories, adventure and mystery stories, and blood and thunder literature. Some sex differences are noted, but are not always evident.

READING INTERESTS

7 years.   Realistic stories (especially boys).
              Animal stories.
              Stories about home life (especially girls).
              Fairy tales (especially girls).
              Funny stories.
              School stories.

9 to 11 years. Heroic, mystery and adventure stories.
              Myths and legends (especially girls).
              Elementary scientific literature (especially boys).
              Books about hobbies (especially boys).

86 MODERN CHILD PSYCHOLOGY

ABILITIES

Boys and girls tend to show some differences in abilities as well as in interests at this stage. These are not so clear cut as at adolescence, and selection for the appropriate type of secondary education—grammar, technical, or modern—is much easier at thirteen years than at eleven years.

We have seen how girls tend to show a more rapid development of speech than boys. This superiority is maintained in all English subjects—oral and written composition, grammar, spelling, and often in geography and history. They seem to express themselves more easily than boys, perhaps because they feel more intensely and their emotions are more readily expressed. They also learn foreign languages more quickly than boys very often; partly because they tend to be more imitative.

Boys, on the other hand, show greater facility in handling number concepts, and usually enjoy mathematical subjects more than girls, perhaps because their approach is more objective and less personal, and they find logical and abstract concepts more interesting than girls. Boys' greater interest and facility in science, physics, chemistry, biology, engineering, is widely recognized—again indicative of a more impersonal and mechanical approach. Boys may also tend to identify themselves with all forms of power as an attempt to fulfil their manhood. Nearly every small boy wants to be an engine driver or a pilot at eight years old; while at fifteen he may strive to be a research chemist or an electrical engineer.

To some extent intellectual curiosity may be derived from normal sexual curiosity—probably more so in boys than in girls. Opportunities for elementary scientific experiments, biological studies, and observation of wild life should be made possible for all boys and girls. Children have a natural interest in animals, birds, flowers and all country things. It is tragic when city-bred children have little or no opportunity to satisfy this interest. Camp schools of the future may do something to redress this wrong.

Five years of age is the compulsory age for school attendance in this country. This assumes that a child of this age is ready for formal education. In actual fact, there are few children

NORMAL DEVELOPMENT OF THE CHILD 87

of five years of age who are really ready, and nowadays the tendency is to introduce formal work in the three Rs towards the end of the fifth year. In America, in some states, attendance is not compulsory until six years of age, which is a much better age for *formal* education.

CHARACTERISTICS OF DEVELOPMENT

However, at this age, a very definite intellectual development takes place. It seems that the child, having a richer vocabulary and greater facility in the use of words, can deal with abstractions more easily. *Thought becomes more abstract* and *less concrete. The child can generalize more quickly* and follow a logical argument more easily. Emotional issues are less in the forefront of the mind and the child's intellectual curiosity is at its height. *His memory span is longer* and *his attentivity greater.* His interests and his field of experimentation are wider.

Intellectual development will, of course, not be so advanced if the child is still much concerned with his own emotional conflicts, if he is still struggling with early emotional difficulties. Anxiety impedes thought. Clarity of thought depends greatly on freedom from neurotic anxiety.

Imitativeness of adults gradually diminishes, though imitation of other children, especially those slightly older, is very marked. They tend to copy each other in speech, dress, mannerisms, tastes and behaviour.

INTELLECTUAL GROWTH

A great many different scales of intelligence tests have been devised for children of school age. I will quote a few examples from well-known scales which show the character of intellectual development between five and eleven years.

Memory Span for Digits	*Memory Span for Sentences*
4 years—4	5 years—12 syllables
7 years—5	8 years—16 syllables
10 years—6	11 years—20 syllables

Definition of Words.

Five years—in terms of use—a stove, "to cook on."

Eight years—in terms of class—a soldier, "a man who shoots."

88 MODERN CHILD PSYCHOLOGY

Eleven years—abstract words such as obedience and revenge can be correctly defined.

Detection of Similarities.

Seven years—similarities between wood and coal, apple and orange can be detected and expressed verbally.

Eight years—both similarities and differences between "cricket ball and orange," "aeroplane and kite," can be detected for instance.

Eleven years—similarities between "rose, potato and tree," or "book, teacher and newspaper," can be given correctly.

Detection of Absurdities

Eight years—"A wheel came off Frank's motor car. As he could not put it on again by himself, he drove his motor car to the garage for repairs." The absurdity here can be correctly stated.

Nine years—"A fireman hurried to the burning house, got his fire hose ready and after smoking a cigarette, began to put out the fire."

Eleven years—"When there is an accident the last carriage of the train is usually damaged most. So they have decided it will be best if the last carriage is always taken off before the train starts."

Reasoning Tests.

Suitable for children between ten and eleven + years.

"Manx cats have short tails. John's cat has a short tail. Is it a Manx cat?"

"Ada sits down on Mary's left, and Ann sits down on Ada's left. If I stand facing them, who is on my right?"

"I am twice as old as my son. Thirty-five years ago I was as old as he is now. What age am I?"

"John is taller than Harry. Dick is not so tall as John. Who is the tallest?"

APPLICATIONS TO EDUCATIONAL METHOD

It is outside the scope of this book to discuss in detail how our knowledge of the facts of child development during this period can best be applied in the classroom. Psychological aspects of educational method will be dealt with in another

NORMAL DEVELOPMENT OF THE CHILD 89

volume in this series. There are, however, certain points which I feel need special emphasis, and I make no apology for introducing them here.

1. *Intellectual development is closely related to emotional development.*
Anxiety interferes with a child's thinking powers considerably. Apprehension prevents good attentivity. Immaturity in emotional development, childishness and over-dependence will handicap learning. Satisfactory intellectual development will follow satisfactory emotional development. Hence the need for emotional outlet in free unorganized play, in rhythmic activity, drawing, creative handicrafts, modelling and acting, especially up to seven or eight years of age, is all important.

2. *Intellectual activity accompanies manipulation and the solution of practical problems.*
Learning by doing is a well-worn educational maxim, and is especially important up to eight years of age. Right through the junior school period the educational milieu may well be practical "centres of interest" in connection with which the tools of learning, reading, writing, and arithmetic can be applied to some purpose. Railways, zoos, circuses, farm life, harvesting, shops, the post office, a newspaper, foreign lands, transport are popular projects which involve all types of handwork and manipulative skills as well as the use of the three Rs. Such methods allow a great deal of free activity and far less sedentary work, which is irksome and unnatural to most children.

3. *Learning must be related to the child's natural interests.*
The first approach to formal work must be associated with things which are real and meaningful to the child. Most reading books nowadays are about people and animals, trains and aeroplanes, and the vocabulary is based on a knowledge of the range and type of the young child's own vocabulary. Pictorial presentation, by the inclusion of illustrations intrinsically interesting to the child is helpful. The first sums include counting—always a delight to a child—giving, sharing

90 MODERN CHILD PSYCHOLOGY

and buying, and the use of concrete material—beads, bricks, counters, pennies, etc.

4. *Interest in technique and mechanics of learning increases with intellectual growth.*

As the child's chronological and mental age increases, so will his facility in handling abstract symbols improve. The phonetic method of teaching reading can best be taught after a mental age of seven. Learning to spell, analysis and synthesis of words, grouping of words becomes of some interest to the child. Even learning multiplication tables if not done in a wholly mechanical way, can be something like an interesting crossword puzzle to the child. The fun of solving a problem provides keen intellectual enjoyment to the normal child, if the arithmetic lesson is not made a drudgery. Any form of puzzle or riddle is intellectual grist to the mind of a child.

5. *The power of memory is keen.*

The junior school child usually learns easily by heart and often enjoys learning jingles, poetry, tables, and spellings. Children make up rhymes on their own initiative. Some children learn more readily by visual methods, by looking at words and figures, and some by auditory methods, saying and hearing them, and others by kinæsthetic methods, writing or tracing letters. The youthful mind is remarkably receptive. Visual aids, the use of the cinematograph in education, auditory aids, the use of the radio and music, have been found to be very helpful especially to the slower child, who finds abstractions difficult to grasp quickly.

6. *There are great individual differences in children's rate of intellectual development.*

The use of intelligence tests has, of course, enabled us to obtain a more reliable knowledge of a child's mental ability than hitherto. We know that children vary greatly in their level of general intelligence and in special abilities. There are quick, slow and just average children, and their special educational needs must be catered for by different methods. Some ways of providing for them are described in a later

NORMAL DEVELOPMENT OF THE CHILD 91

section. Children differ greatly in their rate of learning, and individual methods rather than mass teaching are essential.

SOCIAL DEVELOPMENT

After the hard lessons of social adjustment learnt in the pre-school period, children enjoy much real sociability in the middle years of childhood. Boys tend to choose friends of the same sex; similarly with girls, though combined groups of friends are not uncommon. The social groups are larger than before, although a child has usually one or two close friends or "buddies."

The basis of friendship is often a common interest—cycling, or Red Indian games, or dressing-up. Children often form small clubs or secret societies at this age. Their code is a strict one; rules are usually stringently observed; sometimes an elaborate secret language is devised. Grown-ups are sternly prohibited from interfering and there is obvious pleasure in secret rebellion, and delight in a new-found independence.

This period is sometimes called the "Gang Age"—the peak being put at about eleven years. Of course, gangs can be formed for worthy and unworthy objects, and high spirits and adventuresomeness lead easily into mischief and thence to delinquency.

The juvenile organizations—Scouts, Guides, the Boys' Brigade, and the like—begin to attract the child of about eleven years of age. It seems that the child of this age begins to appreciate good leadership, careful organization and new interests.

It is helpful to be able to play games when the rules are observed and are not rudely broken up by disagreements and quarrelling. The grown-up takes on a new rôle—as inspirer and guide—and the child begins to look outside his family circle for someone on whom to mould himself. He is obviously growing up and away from his family, though the real breakaway—the second weaning—comes at adolescence. Obviously, the part his parents play in his life is all-important. If he feels sure of their affection and support, he is more ready to travel to "fresh fields and pastures new" on his own initiative.

92 MODERN CHILD PSYCHOLOGY

Perhaps growth in independence is the most important single characteristic of the period.

EMOTIONAL DEVELOPMENT

This is sometimes known as the latency period. It implies that the turbulent emotions of the early years are less in evidence and, though checked and controlled, remain latent and dormant, to appear again in a somewhat different form in the turbulence of adolescence.

Certainly there is greater stability and greater control of feelings. Admittedly there are some children who are retarded in emotional development, and there are some who return to babyish behaviour when unduly disturbed by circumstances. This is most pronounced, of course, between five and seven years of age, when the child is learning school adjustment and is often lacking in self-assurance and eager to turn to his parents again for comfort and help. But in general the child learns to put on a brave front and build up a kind of hard shell against the pin-pricks of unkindness and antagonism. He develops much greater reserve towards grown-ups, and often the opinions of his fellows seem to weigh more with him than the opinions of his parents.

Sometimes, of course, there is open rebellion and children delight in defiance and disregard of authority. This needs to be handled wisely if open warfare between the two generations is to be avoided. Much of the behaviour is testing out the parent-child relationship again at a different level. If the parent or teacher can assure the child of his affection, respect and also authority, this stage does not usually last long.

JUVENILE DELINQUENCY

Considerable sociological and psychological study has been made of the subject of juvenile delinquency. As this is a problem which causes a good deal of concern nowadays to parents, teachers, magistrates and welfare workers, it is worth discussing it at some length. Its nuisance value to society is high.

It is sometimes difficult to draw the line between mischief and delinquency. High-spirited youngsters with nowhere to

NORMAL DEVELOPMENT OF THE CHILD 93

play and not much to do will look round for some adventurous sport. They may find tree-climbing sufficient and suffer nothing worse than torn breeches. They may build a bonfire and come home with grimy faces and grimier shirts. They may enjoy chucking pebbles into a pond, but all these activities may lead to destructiveness, damage to property or to persons. In a very restricted neighbourhood, clashes with the police are almost bound to occur.

The solution of this type of delinquency is, of course, to provide the child with sufficient open space, parks, playgrounds, suitable play centres and clubs which give the child that outlet for energetic games and youthful companionship that he needs. Ball games, boxing, swimming, camping, hiking are all very valuable outlets for the lively growing youngster and satisfy his needs well into adolescence.

Delinquency is often explained by the influence of bad companionship, but the companions would not be bad if society provided them with sufficient interesting things to do, and much juvenile delinquency is the fault of society to provide good houses and good play space. The street is not the proper playground for the youngster though its attractions are obvious.

Bad neighbourhood conditions are responsible in some measure, but there are many other factors. In a study[1] made of 200 young delinquents, I found that boys were more numerous than girls, that nine-, ten- and eleven-year-olds were the most numerous, their intelligence tended to be average or slightly below average, that about 50 per cent came from "broken" homes and 50 per cent felt deprived in some way. Their home conditions otherwise tended to be of an average economic standard, and their health was satisfactory in the majority of cases.

The higher incidence of delinquency among males is well known. It is clear that boys are more openly aggressive, more daring and more energetic than girls, and are more likely to get into serious mischief. The ages nine to eleven years represent that period when children are very gregarious and enjoy "gang" activities. They are also more independent and less influenced by the authority of adults. It is a lawless age.

[1]*The Problems of Family Life.* A. H. Bowley. Livingstone, 1946.

94   MODERN CHILD PSYCHOLOGY

Children who feel inferior intellectually, and who are failing in school seek often to compensate by some delinquent activity. This is partly to evade difficulties, e.g. truanting from school, and partly to establish their prestige in the eyes of their fellows. The "broken" home is one disrupted by death, divorce or desertion or patched up by re-marriage or adoption in some cases. In such cases, the child suffers emotionally. He loses his security and the affection he has come to rely on. In my experience, the typical delinquent is one whose mother has died when he was two or three or four, old enough to know her well, and who has been cared for by various well-meaning but unwilling relatives or foster parents. The child is quick to detect that he is unwanted and his delinquency is usually symbolic of his search for affection—he steals what is precious to his mother-substitute.

Another typical case is the illegitimate child whose appearance was resented by his mother and whose presence is unwillingly accepted by his stepfather. He often feels both deprived and aggressive and seeks to revenge himself on society.

The child brought up in an institution after a babyhood spent with different relatives whose methods and whose interest in his well-being varied considerably, is likely to become delinquent. Pilfering is very common in institutions. It is not, I think, due to a "criminal inheritance," but to an acute lack of affection or contact with any loving and cherishing person. It is, I think, obvious that this failure to establish a close contact and attachment to an adult whose approval is sought, whose love is returned and whose solicitude is expected, is the tragedy of the young delinquent.

Deprived children tend to become delinquent. If a child is unloved, he feels unworthy and "a bad object." He may react by the philosophy of "I care for nobody, no not I, and nobody cares for me," and seeks to revenge himself against society. The more he is punished the more bitter and revengeful he feels, and his grudge against the world grows like a snowball.

He may react by accepting his reputation as unlovable and by living up to it. Nothing he can do will be good. His badness and hatefulness is inevitable. His psychological condition is a serious one.

NORMAL DEVELOPMENT OF THE CHILD   95

The child who "steals" love, usually in the form of money, from his parents will continue to do so until he either discovers that their love is not altogether withheld or that despite his badness he will not be punished as severely as his unconscious mind imagines—destroyed, drowned, burned, damaged, in exaggerated unconscious terms, or that someone is strong and wise enough to control his anti-social impulses. It is no help to a child to allow his impulses to remain unchecked. He seeks control and restraint; he must prove to himself that he is not at the mercy of his own violent aggressive urges and that they cannot get the better of him.

He needs restraint and support, therefore, but he also needs a socially acceptable outlet for his aggression in play and sport. He needs the security of a home which bestows appreciation and recognition on him. Without this he cannot grow into a happy and orderly citizen.

In adolescence the child's delinquency may assume a more serious character. He tends to be more rebellious, more independent and more impulsive. He is inwardly disturbed and his impulses clamour for assuagement. His uncertainty and curiosity about sex may lead him into experimentations and a search for sexual experience. Half-ignorant, easily excited, inquisitive, the young person can readily be led astray and needs the guidance and inspiration of an older and wiser person.

It is not then the poverty of the home that matters so much as the warmth of affection and the stability of family life, while outside interests and occupations should provide the child with the intellectual and social stimulus he needs.

CHAPTER IV

THE YOUNG PERSON IN SOCIETY

S Y B I L is thirteen and a half years old and of average intelligence. Her mother complains that she sits about at home reading or listening to the radio, usually highbrow music, instead of going out with other girls. She gets depressed rather often, and complains rather frequently of vague aches and pains, and is always imagining that she has some illness.

She has rather an unusual health history. She had a difficult birth followed by concussion. She developed spastic hemiplegia of the left side diagnosed at eighteen months. This is hardly noticeable now, but she has a slight limp and cannot use her left hand freely. She seems to accept the handicap quite philosophically although it prevents her from dancing or doing physical training. I think she is a little sensitive of her difference from other girls, and is self-conscious when out with them. On the other hand she enjoys riding pillion on her father's motor bicycle. But she does not find it easy to get on with him, dislikes his horse play, and resents his "bossiness."

She is a great reader and good at all English subjects. She would like to work in an office when she leaves school, but is worried lest she cannot do the typing.

She has been given adequate sex education, but says she dislikes "learning about the body," and feels "squeamish" about biology lessons.

Sybil gives a picture of a normal adolescent, whose physical handicap and the natural physical changes of adolescence have caused her to focus attention on physical ailments unduly. She is still too dependent on her parents, perhaps because of her disability and also because she is an only child.

Kenneth is a very clever boy of twelve and a half (I.Q. 126). He is very independent and adventuresome and shows good

96

NORMAL DEVELOPMENT OF THE CHILD 97

initiative. He is very daring and gets involved in all sorts of mischievous enterprises. He has a genius for collecting detentions at school, and was nearly expelled from his secondary grammar school because of his misbehaviour and failure to work hard enough. He is a great stamp collector, enjoys woodwork and gardening sometimes. He is a member of the Scouts and enjoys cycling and camping holidays. He is rather lonely as he has no brothers and sisters, and his school friends do not live near him.

Both his parents work and they have very comfortable means and live in a nice semi-detached house. They have been so anxious not to pamper Kenneth as he is an only child, that it is doubtful if he has had enough affectionate care in babyhood. It is significant that he even now sucks his thumb or bites his nails sometimes.

He is said to have been a difficult and unruly child from birth, always full of high spirits and up to some mischief. He has been involved in a number of minor accidents which required hospital treatment, a cut head, a broken leg, and a poisoned hand. The full physical changes of adolescence have not yet taken place.

His parents expect rather too high a standard and he is left rather too much to his own devices. He has, however, some sterling qualities and should make a fairly good adjustment in the end.

Eileen, twelve and a half years of age and of average intelligence, was finding the beginning of adolescence rather trying. She had lost both her parents, her father in babyhood, and her mother of T.B. when Eileen was nine years old. Her stepfather had never taken much interest in her, and his relatives frankly could not be bothered with her.

Her grandparents had had charge of her since she was ten years old. They did not seem to understand her, nor bother about her much. They complained that she was unreliable, brought back short change from errands, occasionally helped herself to pretty things on her granny's dressing-table, and would take cod liver oil and malt and fruit salts which belonged to other members of the household! The grandmother said she was lazy and did not take enough trouble

G

98   MODERN CHILD PSYCHOLOGY

about her health or hygiene. She also complained that Eileen was too interested in the boys and in the cinema. Also that she was overdramatic and would threaten to commit suicide if she was punished.

When talking to Eileen I formed the impression that she was an unhappy, over-emotional and rather childish young person at heart though with a veneer of sophistication. She liked to play Ludo with her girl friend, and said she "had no use for boys." She was still much of a schoolgirl,, and had no idea what she would like to do when she left, except perhaps to be a ballet dancer. On the other hand she loved dressing-up and trying out new hair styles, and rather liked housework.

I think she felt rather unwanted and abandoned at a most important stage of her life. The suicidal threats which were never serious, were to dramatize the situation at home, and had the desired effect. The grandmother threatened to send her to a home, and Eileen dreaded this threat being put into effect. She was rather a pathetic little figure with dark tragic eyes, outwardly so self-possessed, and inwardly so insecure. Adolescence was likely to be a difficult period of her life, and she needed a good deal of help.

Such children are ordinary children growing up and suffering rather severe growing pains. Many other examples could be cited, but they present a familiar enough picture to parents, teachers, and youth leaders.

The period of adolescence, from eleven to eighteen years, is that stage of development when the child reaches early maturity —preliminary to adulthood.

It is a most interesting time both to the child and to the observer, but can often be a trying time to everyone concerned.

The period is a long one because the physical changes are very variable and may occur at any time between eleven and sixteen years. Girls usually mature earlier than boys. We know that quite definite physical changes take place and that certain glands become active and pour secretions into the blood stream. This has a disturbing effect on the young person who is dimly aware of increased lethargy or excessive vitality, considerable growth in general, a change of voice, and the

NORMAL DEVELOPMENT OF THE CHILD 99

commencement of nocturnal emissions in the boy, breast development and the beginning of menstruation in the girl.

EMOTIONAL DEVELOPMENT

Even though both the boy and the girl have been prepared beforehand, the onset of puberty is often rather strange and puzzling to the young person. The psycho-somatic condition of the organism is obviously disturbed and we may expect certain emotional effects.

The most marked features are the irritability and mood swings of the individual. Feelings are once again very much in the picture and feeling tone can swing from despair to elation very rapidly. Trifles appear to upset the young person unduly and he or she is notably "touchy," and "on edge."

The young person becomes aware of himself in a new light. He is often introspective and highly critical. He varies from exaggerated self-confidence and swagger to a sense of inferiority and bashfulness. He begins to measure himself against adults or people of his own age and becomes sadly aware of his own limitations.

SOCIAL DEVELOPMENT

His relations with his parents usually undergo a definite change. His idols are found to have feet of clay. He scrutinizes and criticizes his parents; he flouts their opinions, and disregards their authority. He challenges their traditional beliefs and takes up Communism and Agnosticism or Dialectical Materialism. This is all expressive of his urgent need to grow up and to find his own feet. If his relationship with his parents has been satisfactory, this phase will have but temporary repercussions.

At the same time he is looking for guidance and support from outside the family. He may turn to the Church for help and become earnestly religious for a time. He may "identify" himself with one of his teachers and show great respect and affection for him. Or he may seek to ape a film star or a famous footballer, and "hitch his wagon to a star." This stage of *hero-worship* is valuable in that he gains new inspiration, new ideas and new interests, but he may suffer sad disillusionment and he may follow impossible ideals and lose touch with

100   MODERN CHILD PSYCHOLOGY

reality and real values. If his home life has been unhappy, he will seek compensation even more now. He may evade difficulties and search for the impossible. He may have day-dreams of great wealth, thrilling adventure or romantic attachments. This is natural enough, but by degrees he should wake up from his day-dreaming and settle down to realizing some part of his ambitions. An older friend can help him a good deal. The child needs companions of his own age to give him the security and support which only they can give. He feels less shy, less different from other people, and more confident in his approach to society when he is surrounded by his own clan, as it were. Youth Centres are usually very popular and young people enjoy mixing with each other. Mixed dances and games are much appreciated. Mutual interests in dramatics, or literature, or in hobbies such as painting, drawing, bird-watching, camping, cycling, are discovered. Friendships with members of the opposite sex spring up and boys and girls learn a good deal about their differences and likenesses. Fleeting love-affairs occur, and much emotion is expressed and experienced. The young person is learning the difficult art of hetero-sexual adjustment. There is safety in numbers and the wider and richer social experience an adolescent can have, the greater his chance of building up good relationships with other people.

The solitary, bookish, morose adolescent is obviously in difficulties. Similarly, the flighty, hyper-active, restless, discontented young person is inwardly ill-at-ease, but there are great individual differences.

One of the most important adjustments the youth has to make during these years is *adjustment to work*. It is easy to find highly paid jobs when manpower is scarce, jobs without any technical training and which lead to nothing permanent. The war has increased this tendency, but fortunately, the new Education Act will see to it that all young people undergo some further education whether academic, cultural or technical. In America, they seem able to offer better educational facilities than in Great Britain. It is the custom to stay at school until seventeen or eighteen years of age, and a large number of boys and girls go to junior colleges. Here they can learn every-

NORMAL DEVELOPMENT OF THE CHILD 101

thing from beauty parlour training to business management and the classics! In some districts they alternate between three months in college and three months in a job, and in this way they discover where their abilities lie, and improve their knowledge at the same time. With part-time education we may achieve equally good results.

It is obvious that handicapped children need more guidance than others, and education authorities usually provide some after-care service, but most folk need some vocational guidance, and Juvenile Employment Bureaux, teachers and parents can aid them; expert psychological advice and vocational guidance can also be very helpful. The psychological factors behind maladjustment in work are many. The child may be still unweaned in the psychological sense. He may still be looking for worthy parental substitutes, still need a mother and be unduly dependent. (This tendency will also wreck a marriage relationship incidentally.) He seeks a sheltered post and cannot take much responsibility or show initiative readily.

Another child seeks to revolt from parental chains and reacts exaggeratedly in the opposite direction. He objects to supervision or advice or criticism and proves truculent and difficult unless allowed to be responsible or assume leadership.

Still another child may identify himself with one of his parents and seek to emulate him in some vocation to which he is quite unsuited. Sometimes, of course, he is urged into the parental occupation to please his parents or satisfy their ambitions.

Some people are a little obsessional and seek a safe, routinized job. Some are over-anxious and need a sympathetic employer. Some have not learnt to work *with* people, but work well with things and do satisfactory factory work. Some are natural leaders, while others tend to follow contentedly. Obviously it takes all sorts to make a world, and we need both our dustmen and our professors. We need to guard against neurotic motives in the choice of a career. Has the actress fallen in love with herself, and is she a prey to self-exhibitionism? Does the philanthropist or welfare worker seek to "do good" from an excessive feeling of "guilt"? These are searching questions.

102   MODERN CHILD PSYCHOLOGY

INTELLECTUAL DEVELOPMENT

During these years there is a tremendous intellectual awakening. Scientific curiosity is at its height. Literature may be appreciated for the first time. Artistic ability may flower. Mechanical aptitude may be apparent. A special gift for languages or music may be recognized. It is the task of secondary education to stimulate special abilities and to satisfy the young person's educational needs. It is a kind of intellectual renaissance, and if full use is made of a tremendous opportunity, great intellectual advancement takes place. Thought becomes more abstract. The vocabulary widens. There is greater facility in the use of language. Debates and discussions can be greatly enjoyed. Literary and dramatic societies flourish abundantly. Some young people can express themselves in drawing, some in writing, and some in talking, but it is obvious that they need some real outlet for expression. This will serve to sublimate emotions and so to control and guide them. This will prove a safety valve and the adolescent who writes poems or reads love stories avidly is not a fit subject for ridicule. Nature points the way.

Unfortunately, many important examinations take place at this time, and sometimes the adolescent cannot do justice to himself. He may be suffering from emotional strain and find difficulty in clarity of thinking. Breakdowns are, of course, not uncommon at adolescence. The strain upon the whole organism is considerable, and the tendency of the young adolescent to "laze" and "lounge" and "mope" about is natural enough.

Earlier in this book I gave an account of reading preferences of children between twelve and fifteen years. We saw that the older boy reads rather more detective stories, more historical stories and technical books, fewer school stories and those about home life, while his enjoyment of adventure stories remains fairly constant. Girls, as they grow older, read more love stories, more historical stories, plays, and poetry. Their interest in school and home stories decreases, but adventure stories remain popular.

Psychologically, children tend to read partly as a compensation—to make up for a commonplace life, partly as a

NORMAL DEVELOPMENT OF THE CHILD 103

release—to identify themselves with the heroes and heroines of the story, and partly for inspiration and relaxation. It is, on the whole, wisest to refrain from interference as regards the child's choice of books. He has to work through the childish stage, the "blood and thunder" stage, and the erotic stage. He needs this form of escape and occasional relief from the labours of growing-up. Gradually if he has access to alternative literature, at home, at school, and in the public library, his reading interests may begin to show a higher cultural level. Parents and teachers tend to be over critical. I know of one family where the father complains because his thirteen-year-old son will read the *Wizard* and *Hotspur*, while the mother cannot understand how he can enjoy *David Copperfield*!

The cinema and the radio may exert a powerful influence over the tastes of young people during this stage of development. The cinema has rather a pernicious influence in that it provides ready-made passive enjoyment requiring no effort on the part of the beholder. Amateur dramatics or a game of tennis are more valuable. On the other hand, films provide an escape, a relaxation, and a safety valve for emotion which tends to be excessive in adolescence. As long as the cinema does not act as too powerful a drug, it does not, I think, hurt the working-class boy or girl very greatly to see beautiful clothes and furnishings and food, exciting events and handsome young men gazing at ravishing females. I doubt very much whether cinema-going really influences the incidence of juvenile delinquency to any extent. It is only if the underlying discontent and conflict is already latent that a crime picture may present the idea rather too forcefully to the boy or girl. Very probably he or she would have become delinquent in any case if the nuclear problem was already there.

Films can, of course, have a very valuable educational effect, and many documentary, historical, classical or epic shows are much appreciated by adolescents.

The radio again has been described as "canned enjoyment," in that it provides effortless pleasure, and encourages the natural laziness and apathy of the adolescent. Certainly it can provide real enjoyment which is surely of value in these hard-

104 MODERN CHILD PSYCHOLOGY

pressed days of modern life. It is also educational in the widest
sense. It will "start you talking," teach you old-time dances,
spelling, general knowledge, Bridge leads, ancient and modern
tunes and all the newest jokes! If listened to with intelligence
and discrimination, a young person can gain a great deal of
pleasure and knowledge.

Provided other outlets in athletics, dancing, dramatics,
community singing, social gatherings, and so on, are sought,
neither the cinema nor the radio can do much harm, and one
must remember that the lively restless adolescent will not be
content with passive enjoyment for long.

Extension of the school-leaving age will provide education
authorities with the task of providing young people with the
intellectual, social and emotional satisfactions they need through
further education. Prolonged cultural and liberal education can
be of immense benefit if presented in a way which appeals to
a growing young person who feels usually rather sophisticated,
worldly-minded and a little superior. Further technical education related in some measure to the work the youth is taking
up, can be equally beneficial if its relevance and realistic nature
is apparent.

Bearing in mind the normal characteristics of adolescents,
perhaps the following points might be helpful to remember
for those of us who are required to plan further education.

1. *The desire for responsibility.*
Adolescents like to manage things for themselves, to
organize discussions, arrange demonstrations, to plan and to
execute without too much adult assistance.

2. *The tendency to be irresponsible.*
At the same time youth likes to feel thoroughly carefree
and irresponsible sometimes, and should be able to rely
on grown-ups in the background to take responsibility now
and again for them.

3. *Impatient for results.*
Patient painstaking work towards a far-distant goal only
comes with maturity. Young people need to feel that the ends

NORMAL DEVELOPMENT OF THE CHILD 105

for which they are striving can be achieved in a not too distant future. Carelessness, hurry, superficiality, are all characteristics of this age, and no amount of scolding or retribution will greatly influence these traits until the child himself recognizes the need for reform.

4. *Enthusiasm.*

Adolescents notably are enthusiastic and their zeal should be directed to some worthwhile end. The desire to alleviate distress, to reform, to build a new heaven upon earth is present in almost every young person, and this can be harnessed to some purpose. Many valuable lessons in citizenship can be learned if they are made sufficiently practical and appropriate. Enthusiasm for nature, for a good poem, a fine drama, a beautiful costume, an efficient machine should always be encouraged, never scorned, even though adolescent tastes may change in a few weeks.

5. *Adult interests.*

Although the adolescent will be childish, flippant, off-hand, bored, and foolish at times, he is very much aware and interested in his approaching adulthood, and his education should seek to give him further information, and inspiration concerning more mature interests. Perhaps the most obvious way by which this can be done for the girl is to teach her something about homemaking and mothercraft, personal hygiene and beauty culture. This will normally be of real interest to her and fulfil an obvious need. In the case of boys particularly, the medieval practice of apprenticeship to a craftsman had much to commend it. It is obviously best to learn about a trade or a craft by watching an expert and trying alongside him. Contact with adults, who are themselves artists, craftsmen, skilled workers of any kind can be very beneficial to young people. It is unfortunate that so much of modern industry requires only unskilled and mechanical labour.

The approach of the teacher to the whole question of further education is of the greatest importance. The young people should be thought of as students striving to discover things for themselves with the aid of experts, rather than pupils whose immature minds need to be moulded or driven.

106   MODERN CHILD PSYCHOLOGY

We are likely to see much interesting experimental work in adolescent and adult education in the years to come.

REFERENCES

1. Bayley, N.	*The California Infant Scale of Motor Development*	Univ. of Calif. Press, 1936
2. Blatz, W. E. & Bott, H.	*The Management of Young Children*	Dent, 1931
3. Bowley, A. H.	*The Natural Development of the Child*	Livingstone, 1940
4. Bühler, C. & Metzer, H.	*Testing Children's Development*	Allen & Unwin, 1935
5. Gesell, A.	*The First Five Years of Life.*	Methuen, 1941
	The Mental Growth of the Pre-School Child	Macmillan, 1925
6. Hazlitt, V.	*Infancy*	Methuen, 1933
7. Hollingworth, L. S.	*The Psychology of the Adolescent*	King, 1930
8. Isaacs, S.	*The Nursery Years*	Routledge, 1929
	Intellectual Growth in Young Children	Routledge, 1930
	Social Development in Young Children	Routledge, 1933
9. Kenwrick, E. & H.	*The Child from Five to Ten*	Kegan Paul, 1930
10. Lewis, M. M.	*Infant Speech*	
11. MacCalman, D. P.	*Advances to Understanding the Adolescent*	Home and School Council, 1938
12. Shirley, M.	*The First Two Years* (3 Vols.)	Univ. of Minn. Press, 1933
13. Shinn, M.	*Biography of a Baby*	Univ. Press, Berkeley, 1909
14. Stutsman, P.	*Mental Measurement of the Pre-School Child*	Harrap, 1931
15. Terman, L., & Merrill, M.	*Measuring Intelligence*	Harrap, 1937
16. Wagoner, L. C.	*Development of Learning in Young Children*	McGraw Hill Book Co., London, 1933

SECTION III

GROWTH AND DEVELOPMENT DURING THE FIRST YEAR

NORMS FROM GESELL, BÜHLER, SHINN AND BAYLEY

	First Month	Third Month	Sixth Month	Ninth Month	One Year
Gross Motor Development. *Locomotion.*	Holds head erect now and then. Turns head to look.	Holds head steady. Kicks feet in bath.	Sits with slight support. Rolls back to stomach. Splashes with hands and feet in bath.	Crawls. Can roll. Will make stepping movements if held.	Stands. Walks with support. Can climb up and down stairs.
Fine Motor Co-ordination.	Grasps finger.	Plays with hands. Clasps small cube.	Co-ordinates what is seen with what is felt. Can clutch at a dangling ring. Turns head to bell.	Handling more accurate. Manipulates with one hand. Can hold two bricks. Will try to put a brick into a hole in a board.	Can hold a cup to drink from. Can oppose thumb to finger in grasping. Can build a tower of two bricks.
Perceptual Development.	Reacts to bright light.	Eyes follow moving person.		Reaches directly for a spoon and for string.	Can replace circle in inset in form board. Shows preference for coloured, rather than plain figures.

	First Month	Third Month	Sixth Month	Ninth Month	One Year
Vocalization.	Cries of hunger. etc.	Some vocalization.	Much crowing and babbling. Articulates syllables. Reacts to music.	Most consonant and vowel sounds distinguishable.	Can say two or three words. Imitates sounds. Vocalizes to music. Adjusts to words.
Adaptive Behaviour.		Adapts to nursing. Recognizes signs of nursing. Reacts to paper on face. Hands react to table.	Can bang spoon and manipulate it in cup and saucer. Expresses recognition. Lifts inverted cup to find brick.	Imitates actions. Pats table. Looks for fallen spoon. Puts bottle in mouth.	Can pick up brick after finding it under cup. Uses string to secure dangling object. Unwraps brick hidden in paper. Rings bell in imitation.
Social-Emotional Behaviour.	Anger, fear. Affection distinguishable.	Jealousy can be detected. Pays selective attention to faces. Recognizes familiar persons.	Distinguishes strangers. Shows hostility to them. Frolics when played with.	Reacts to mirror-image. Waves bye-bye. Plays peek-a-boo. Enjoys company.	Very dependent on mother. Welcomes strangers. Inhibits on command. Helps when being dressed. Thumb-sucking is common.

GROWTH AND DEVELOPMENT DURING 2 - 5 YEARS

NORMS FROM GESELL, BÜHLER, STUTSMAN, TERMAN AND MERRILL

	Second Year	Third Year	Fourth Year	Fifth Year
Gross Motor Development.	Walks without help. Can run, jump and climb. Can ride a Kiddy-car.	Locomotion now steadier and speedier. Can skip, hop and stand on one foot.	Free and active movement. Responds well to music.	
Fine Motor Co-ordination.	Can build a tower of six bricks. Can cut with scissors. Can fasten large buttons.	Can copy a cross. Can place round pegs in round holes and square pegs in square holes.	Can copy a square.	Can copy a star. Can tie a knot.
Perceptual Development.	Can match colours (2 yrs.). Enjoys looking at pictures. Identifies self in mirror.	Can fit a nest of boxes.	Can match shapes. Can distinguish similarities and differences.	Can name highly saturated colours.
Vocalization.	Vocabulary about 200 words. Uses a few words to convey meaning of whole sentence.	Vocabulary about 890 words. Can follow simple commands. Asks frequent questions.	Can use a complete sentence (about six to eight words in length).	Vocabulary 2,000 to 3,000 words. Can define familiar words, e.g. hat, ball, stone.
Adaptive Behaviour.	Bowel and bladder control should be established.	Can draw a rudimentary man. Can build a block bridge. Can string beads.	Can repeat four digits.	Can count four objects. Can draw a man with body, neck, head, arms and legs.
Social and Emotional Behaviour.	Usually indifferent or hostile to others. Dependent on adults. Tantrums rather common.	Often aggressive to others. Rather quarrelsome. Less dependent on adults. Night-terrors, stammering, food fads rather common.	More co-operative and friendly with adults and children. Can be both a leader and a follower. Is willing to share and take turns.	Can make an effective social adjustment. Emotions more controlled. Good independence.

SECTION IV

CHAPTER I

PSYCHO-ANALYTIC THEORY AND METHOD IN RELATION TO EARLY DEVELOPMENT DURING THE FIRST TWO YEARS

T H E practice and theory of psycho-analysis has given a deeper significance and a different evaluation to the facts of child behaviour. The descriptive and observational items of behaviour recorded by Preyer, Scupin, Stern, Gesell, Bühler, Valentine, and others have been integrated and shown in their true importance by the work of psycho-analysis. The careful observations of healthy, normal and well-cared-for infants, such as those undertaken by Bühler (1), Middlemore (13), Shepherd (16), and Shirley (17), have provided valuable evidence of the behaviour of infants and psycho-analytic studies have given a fuller meaning to such observations. Now it has been said that psycho-analytic views are based upon a convergence of evidence, clinical evidence, observational data and integration of certain well-established facts and theories. This evidence is open to investigation by anyone who has the patience and interest to examine the literature. For many people this is not possible, and in this section I am attempting the somewhat ambitious task of summarizing the findings of psycho-analysts in regard to the first six months, and then in regard to the first and second year of life. Naturally, this is my own rendering of the facts and theories put forward by well-known psycho-analysts, and is open to charges of mis-interpretation and misunderstanding. I have had access to some unpublished material and to technical writings which are not generally available to the lay reader. Although some of the material is rather controversial and theoretical, the findings of this body of workers appears to me to be so important that I feel it is worth while to try to make them intelligible to the general public in order to give them a fuller understanding of child development, and to attempt to reduce

114 MODERN CHILD PSYCHOLOGY

some of the mistakes made in child management. I shall avoid material which is very controversial or highly theoretical, and, wherever possible, use simple terms in place of technical ones, and give full explanations of the less familiar concepts.

OBSERVATIONAL DATA

First, I will list certain well-known facts of development which have already been mentioned in this book, and to which psycho-analysts have given a fuller meaning, and regard as evidence of the truth of their theoretical standpoint.

The relative predominance of negative expressional movements and sounds over positive ones during the first two months of life.

The relative predominance of flight and defence reactions to too loud, bright or painful stimuli during the first few months of life over responsive and positive reactions.

The expression of strong emotion in relation to the feeding situation.

The frequency with which healthy, normal infants may bite the breast, even before the appearance of teeth, as well as the numerous occasions when he may smile or show signs of pleasure and affection.

The greater range and variety of activity enjoyed by a six-months-old infant, and the increased skill in handling and reaching which can be observed.

The attention paid to the features—mouth, eyes, nose, hair—of the individual who feeds him.

The ability of the six-months-old child to distinguish between familiar persons and strangers, and the hostility or sullenness often apparent towards strangers.

The relative dependence of the year-old child on his parents and the anxiety shown when the parents leave the child for any length of time.

The increase in skills, activities, and mobility which walking brings about.

The frequency of tantrums observed in the two-year-old.

The jealousy shown towards the father or brothers and sisters in the family.

PSYCHO-ANALYTIC THEORY AND METHOD 115

The nature of the young child's play, e.g. destructiveness, aggressive traits, feeding games with dolls, play involving losing and finding, peek-a-boo, hide-and-seek, hunt-the-thimble, etc.

The prevalence of feeding difficulties between three and five years.

The content of phobias and night-terrors which are especially common at about three years of age.

The prevalence of incontinence and frequency of micturition in the pre-school years.

The hostility and antagonism shown towards other children at times, especially to younger children or strange children.

The gradual acquirement of skill in action and speech by the pre-school child.

The greater stability and emotional control shown by the school child.

Many more facts and detailed items of behaviour could be given; I have merely listed those with which I am most familiar, either from reported observations or from my own experience of children of all ages.

The work of psycho-analysis is no longer in its infancy. Freud's important writings based on psycho-analysis of adults has thrown light on the nature of thought and feeling in infancy, and his work has had a profound influence on the whole of child psychology. It has remained for the English group of psycho-analysts to further the study of very young children, and the writings of Klein and Isaacs are probably the most important in this connection. Children as young as two years onwards have been analysed, and their symptoms and their behaviour during psycho-analysis has thrown a new light on the early development of children.

It is, therefore, important that I should try to give some account of the methods by which the conclusions of psycho-analysis are reached. Isaacs writes, "Scepticism is sometimes expressed as to the possibility of understanding the psychic life at all in the earliest years—as distinct from observing the sequence and development of behaviour. In fact, we are far from having to rely upon mere imagination

116　　MODERN CHILD PSYCHOLOGY

or blind guess-work, even as regards the first year of life. When all the observable facts of behaviour are considered in the light of analytic knowledge gained from adults, and children over two years, and are brought into relation with analytic principles, we arrive at many hypotheses carrying a high degree of probability and some certainties, regarding early mental processes.[1]"

We have, then, the evidence provided by non-analytic observations and experimental studies, to which I have devoted a great part of this book, on the one hand. On the other hand, we have the evidence gained by analysts from the actual analysis of adults and children. This evidence can be checked by the recognition of the accuracy of interpretations made during the analysis. The analysand recognizes that the "cap fits." Moreover, following interpretation, the character of the individual's play or behaviour may change; memories of past experience may be recovered; and affective responses are apparent; unconscious material may become conscious. Again, repetition occurs—the same essential situation—always slightly different, but with the same general structure, is brought up by every patient. Moreover, the symptoms disappear, the anxieties diminish, intellectual energy is liberated and the patient gets well. The successful analysand can bear witness to these facts. This is a very bare summary of the evidence. It must be remembered that the analyst pays great attention to detail, of speech, and behaviour of the patient, is careful to note the context of particular data in the mental life of the individual, and recognizes any particular data to be part of a developmental process, i.e. "To regard each manifestation at any given time and in any given situation as a member of a developing series whose rudimentary beginnings can be traced backwards and whose further, more mature, forms can be followed forwards." Also the "transference" which the patient established towards the analyst, his emotional relationship to the analyst, reveals in a most vivid and dramatic way situations of feeling and impulse, and mental processes generally, which have been experienced earlier on in his relationships to people in his external life and

[1]From MSS. to be published.

PSYCHO-ANALYTIC THEORY AND METHOD 117

personal history. He transfers his early wishes, aggressive impulses, fears and other emotions on to the analyst. The patient re-lives his infantile experiences, and is carried back far beyond the earliest conscious memories.

We must also remember that analytic studies are highly intensive and provide a vast amount of detailed material about one individual. "It is a misleading prejudice in the psychological field, brought from the physical sciences, to assume that number of cases is more important than conditions and detail of observation. If, instead of persons, we consider actual wealth of data, variety of situation, even mere hours of observation, then our work may claim a high quantitative status" (p. 160).[1] (8)

THE FIRST SIX MONTHS OF LIFE

Probably the first important and disturbing experience of the infant is his separation from his mother at birth. This will constitute his first *experience of loss*. It is an experience which every individual must suffer, and no doubt provides some degree of shock and disturbance to every infant. It is clear that when the infant becomes separated from his mother at birth she will be his first main object of love and desire which he will seek to recover.

His subsequent experience of the mother is through his contact at the breast when he is suckling. At first the whole interest and love focus on the nipple and on the breast, but soon interest develops in the face and in the hands which attend and gratify him. The young infant, as we have noticed, attends to his mother's breast, sucking at it, patting it, feeling it, and biting at it. He also begins early to pay selective attention to her face. His range of vision is very limited in these early days, and these objects must surely come into focus most often when he is awake.

During the first two months, of course, a great part of the infant's life is spent in sleeping. During his waking periods he is mainly concerned with feeding, and the breast is the main focus of attention. His first satisfactions and frustrations

[1]Isaacs, S. *Criteria for Interpretation*. Int. J. of P.A., Vol. XX, Pt. II. April, 1939.

118 MODERN CHILD PSYCHOLOGY

are related to it; his first emotions are experienced in regard to it; his first intellectual awareness appears associated with it; and his first attempts at speech are usually in relation to the feeding situation. Clearly it is a matter of life and death to him. Greed, natural hunger, the life instinct, the instinct of self-preservation, call it what you will, is the primary impulse of the infant. Denial of this satisfaction, frustration, delay, or postponement must certainly seem like physical and psychic death to the infant.

One must assume then that there is a very real fear of a loss of the breast and consequently a desire to control or possess the breast. The infant's first experience of anxiety must be due to the fear that his mother may not return. Obviously the infant is helpless and solely dependent on the mother's goodwill. He can try to summon her by screaming, but it seems that prolonged screaming is felt to be an aggressive attack on himself by his mother and only increases the anxiety, unless she responds immediately. It is noticeable that almost the earliest form of play is connected with losing and finding objects, throwing things out of the pram and seeking to recover them again. In psycho-analytic terms, this represents an attempt to control and recover the mother.

It is also clear that the very young infant must be greatly taken up with the experience of *internal sensations*. His knowledge, perception, experience and understanding of the external world is very limited, especially before he has learnt to sit up. Some awareness of strong stimuli—light, heat, cold, wetness, sound, movement, and the presence of his mother— the feel of her breast and of her hands, the light and shade on her face and the sound of her voice, is evident, but during the first month his periods of wakefulness are very short. It is natural that internal kinæsthetic sensations appear very important in his life—sensations in the mouth, the alimentary canal, in the stomach, the experience of wind, evacuation of the bowels and of the bladder, the feel of his clothes on his body, and so on. Thus, until he is able to hold his head erect, lift his body or sit up, his world must be mainly limited to himself, his sensations, and, very probably, his phantasies about them.

Until about the eighth or ninth month, the mouth is the

PSYCHO-ANALYTIC THEORY AND METHOD 119

predominant organ of touch. Not only is it used for sucking from the breast or bottle, but it is used to explore the properties of objects in the external world. Everything is conveyed to the mouth, for it appears to be the most sensitive organ at this time and thus he gains more accurate perceptions from its use. This is a fact generally noted by observers. It is evident also that he is anxious when the breast is not forthcoming, and his tendency to bite at the breast has also been noted.

It seems legitimate to assume that the infant seeks to eat up or devour the breast in his greedy desire. By this means he may either be able to retain it and preserve it inside him, and so defend himself against the fear of loss, or in his anger at his frustration and unsatisfied desire he may seek to punish and destroy the "bad" breast, i.e. the "bad" mother who fails to satisfy him immediately. It seems probable that very early the infant begins to build up a concept of a "good" loving, satisfying, kind mother who supplies him with all his wants, and a "bad" hateful, frustrating, even destroying mother, who may seek to destroy or starve him. His own "bad" feelings of anger and hate which are stirred up inside him come to be identified in his own mind with his "bad" mother. When we bear in mind that his main idea in these first months is to take everything inside him, and that his mind is much taken up with the experience of internal sensations, it does not seem surprising that from the point of view of the deepest and most primitive levels of the mind, the child actually feels his mother to be inside him, acting upon him with all the "good" or "bad" qualities which he has experienced in the outside world. This is known technically as the *introjection of the object*. It is a difficult concept to accept or understand because it is so remote from the adult way of thinking, but child analysts have found it to be a universal tendency in the deeper layers of the mind and one which exerts a profound influence on his behaviour. Sucking, i.e. absorption into the body by the mouth is a universal impulse in all human infants. The breast, the bottle, the thumb, the dummy, and a great variety of toys and objects are all sucked with avidity. Frustration of this desire will increase the need to suck and to devour a thousandfold.

120 MODERN CHILD PSYCHOLOGY

It seems logical then to assume that the infant feels he holds inside him either "good" satisfying food or a "good" mother figure, or on the other hand "bad" poisonous food or a "bad" mother figure. The child has a most disturbing situation with which to deal. He now contains a "bad" object within, which may produce "bad" contents and turn his own bodily products, e.g. fæces and urine, into "bad," dangerous objects, capable of harming himself or his mother. Herein lies the cause of anxieties and difficulties over toilet training which are so common in early childhood. The terms "good" and "bad" are used here in a very special sense. They do not refer to moral or real qualitative character but to the infant's own feelings and phantasies and how things seem to him. Furthermore, by devouring the breasts, he fears he will destroy the source of food, the loved object and also give the mother cause for retaliation and vengeance in the terms familiar to his infantile way of thinking—biting, destroying, wetting or burning him with urine. The phantasy of poisonous food is a recurrent theme in fairy tales. I know a little boy of four who was unable to suckle in infancy and had to be fed nasally until he could take the bottle. Feeding difficulties persisted into childhood. At four years of age he appeared an anxious, worried, insecure little boy, always questioning or fretting, or seeming depressed and irritable. He also fretted for his father who was in the Army. I was not surprised to find that in his play he found great pleasure in feeding dolls and teddies with water in a bottle or making wet sand pies for them. This seemed in his case *reparative* play, or play to reassure himself that food was good and non-poisonous. His delight in water play was very marked also.

I do not think any thoughtful observer of young children can doubt the truth of this fact—that very early indeed the child builds up a phantasy of a "bad" attacking mother in his own mind. How else can we explain the fairy tale concept of the wicked witch or the hateful stepmother, usually with long nails, prominent teeth, a large nose and fierce eyes? This aggressive figure is the bogey of the child mind and appears to occur in some degree even in the case of children who have in reality the most loving and kindly of mothers. It is natural

PSYCHO-ANALYTIC THEORY AND METHOD   121

that the infant should think of the mother's attacks in the terms of his own infantile experiences—biting, devouring, starving or deserting. His fear of desertion, starvation or destruction, together with his feeling of helplessness must be especially vivid at this period.

The content of children's later night terrors and phobias are difficult also to explain unless we postulate this conception of an aggressive mother. All observers of young children note the frequency with which little children, especially of two or three years, dream of dangerous, attacking animals and wake in terror with the image of lion or tiger in their minds. In the phobia the child tends to project his inner fear of aggression on to some object in the external world and so strives to ease his inner tension. We see then that *introjection*, the taking in of the dangerous object, and *projection*, the thrusting out of the dangerous feelings, are two ways by which the infant seeks to deal with his early problems.

The so-called *anal* phase arises out of the child's absorption with his inner sensations and digestive processes, and seems evident at a very early age. His bodily products—fæces and urine in particular—may appear "good" or "bad" objects. They are either gifts to please the "good" mother and repair the damage he fears he may have done her, or they are the weapons to attack the "bad" mother and revenge himself on her. There is no doubt that very early indeed the infant recognizes the emotional aura surrounding the processes of elimination. There are few mothers who can preserve an entirely neutral attitude to the whole business of toilet training. "Be a good boy," or "Do your duty" are common nursery phrases. Fæcal incontinence in later years is clearly often a form of retaliation—in particular towards hated stepmothers, I have found—and is a very potent weapon.

Probably this concept of anal aggression and anal eroticism, i.e. love and hate, expressed in bodily terms—is one of the most difficult to accept. We have to peruse psycho-analytic literature and accounts of case-studies to realize how definite this tendency appears to be in infancy. During analysis the adult frequently regresses to this stage and re-lives early anal phantasies. This is quite clearly a fact of clinical experience

122 MODERN CHILD PSYCHOLOGY

and cannot be ignored. Both the analyst and the analysand will bear witness.

A study of early play behaviour, and the general evidence of psycho-analytic findings, provides further evidence. Play commences at the breast and at first consists of manipulation of the mother's breast or body, and later, manipulation and play with his own body. The delight of inserting one thing into another may well be symbolic of *oral* play—putting the nipple into the mouth. Losing and finding objects is probably the infant's way of mastering his anxiety about the loss of the breast or the mother; the "peek-a-boo" and "bye-bye" games which are so popular, help to reassure him that what appears lost and gone away will surely return. The pushing, pulling, reaching play of the older infant is his attempt to master and control his environment and external objects. Gradually, as perception develops, things in the external world become interesting in themselves and his interest in his own movements and sensations which dominate the mental picture right through the first year begin to decrease in the second year.

THE SECOND SIX MONTHS

At *about five or six months*, as we have seen, an important stage in perceptual development is reached. The infant recognizes that what he feels and holds is the same object that he sees. Before this time he does not appear to co-ordinate the two perceptions. At the same time he learns to sit erect for short periods and thus his range of vision and activity is greatly enlarged. Also we have noted that he begins to appreciate the difference between strangers and familiar persons. The child now seems to become aware of his mother as a whole person, external and independent of himself, while before she must have meant little more than a breast to feed him, a face close to him and a pair of arms to enfold him. The child is definitely more of a person by six months, and the external world consists more clearly of persons and things. This represents something of a crisis in the child's life. "It is at this time that he first realizes that those primitive pictures of the 'bad' mother and the 'good' mother are not separate and distinct

PSYCHO-ANALYTIC THEORY AND METHOD   123

entities, but aspects of one and the same person, towards whom he, the child, feels these contrary impulses of love and hate.[1]"

This awareness of his own conflicting feelings towards his own mother is a very disturbing fact indeed to the infant. He has to face the awful truth that he wants to destroy what he loves when he feels angry and hateful towards her. He experiences love, hate, anxiety and guilt in regard to her. Here, then, is the nuclear problem with which every child has to deal—his love and hate for the same person and for the person on whom he is so greatly dependent. He wishes to damage what supports him when he is consumed with infantile rage and hate. This is known as ambivalence—the dual attitude of love and hate which every child feels for his parents. The strength of his hate will, of course, depend greatly on the amount of frustration and denial that he receives, but some of both is inevitable in the bringing up of every child.

We have seen from Bühler's (1), Middlemore's (13), and Shirley's (17) observations that negative expressional movements tend to predominate over the positive ones in the early months of life. These positive movements—handling, reaching, responding, smiling—increase after three months, predominate at five months and markedly predominate at twelve months. Bernfeld (2) says that this is due to the gradual overcoming of anxiety and the increase in the pleasure in positive activities. This clearly coincides with the baby's greater mobility and his greater control of his own body and of his environment. He can manipulate and master things to a greater extent. He can communicate more easily with the adults in his environment and so ensure with greater certainty that they recognize his needs. It must be remembered that the infant has almost no experience or knowledge of time and the loss of the breast or mother in his early days is an absolute one. He feels that not only is the breast that kept him waiting in his intense hunger a bad and dangerous object, because it gives rise to fears of permanent loss, but also he feels angry and hateful towards it, and so to his mother, and he feels frightened about

[1]*On the Bringing-up of Children*, Edited by Rickman, J., p. 176. Kegan Paul, 1936.

124 MODERN CHILD PSYCHOLOGY

these very feelings in himself. As he grows older, his fears and anxieties are greatly eased by his experience of kindness and love from his mother, by the recurrent reappearance of the breast which assuages his hunger, and the constant protection and comfort which his mother's presence affords him. At the same time his gradual mastery of skills, his growth in perceptual awareness, his progress in walking and talking, help him to feel more powerful, and at the same time more worthy and lovable and capable. His belief in the good mother becomes more and more secure as his capacity for active pleasure increases—as well as his perceptions of his actual mother when she ministers to him.

In the second half-year, the infant thus gains much relief from his inner anxiety by turning his fears outwards (projection), by making good in play-ways what he feels he has damaged (reparation), and by directing asocial impulses outward in socially acceptable behaviour, e.g. banging his toys, kicking in the bath, throwing his ball away (sublimation).[1] The development of language provides him not only with a means of communication, but also with a method of winning approval and recognition. His social relationships develop considerably. "The perception of reality acts as a defence against anxiety and as a means of building up trust in his inner world," Isaacs (7).

The infant's relationship to his father is an important one. At first he does not seem to enter into the picture a great deal, but very soon the child must derive a sense of safety and support from the father—the strong person who picks him up and helps him to get what he wants. He must soon feel also recognition and approval and response from the father when he smiles at the child's antics and makes encouraging sounds to him. Again, the father is a person to admire—a strong, clever, capable person who obviously is an important person in the household and one who exerts considerable influence over his mother. Quite early, however, the child must appreciate that the father is to some extent his rival for his

[1]For a fuller account of "defence mechanism" see Anne Freud: *The Psycho-Analytical Treatment of Children*, p. 88. Imago Publishing Co., 1946.

PSYCHO-ANALYTIC THEORY AND METHOD 125

mother's love, that the infant cannot possess the mother entirely, and that the father has strong claims on her. He feels that his father will resent his own claims on the mother, and the child's possession of the mother's breast. The father can be a terrifying figure to the child, one who seeks to punish or harm the child in the familiar, infantile ways, and the child, in his turn, feels antagonistic and angry towards his father—one who steals his mother's love and claims her attention. He will attack the father in play or in phantasy, and yet how frequently he must be made aware of his own impotence and helplessness at the hands of those giants and wizards who are his parents! He builds up inside his mind a picture of his father—a lovable and yet a hateful figure with power to give or take away, heal or harm. This figure acts as a powerful controlling force in his own mind. If it is not too terrifying a figure, he will gradually accept both parental figures as benevolent, controlling influences with power to help him do good and achieve what he wishes—a rudimentary form of conscience or super-ego.

We must remember also that in the early years the child seems to regard his own wishes as extremely powerful with infinite power to do good or ill just as he feels his parents can do to him. If one of his parents falls ill, it is common to find that the child feels as if he were somehow responsible for the parent's illness—as if his own aggressive wishes, which he feels from time to time, have had power to damage his parent. He may feel guilty and desperately anxious. Now there are two special ways by which a child can be helped to over-come these feelings. His good experience of kind, good, real parents will modify his ideas about the imaginary figures in his mind, and phantasy will be tempered by reality. The more certain proof he receives that they will not in reality punish or destroy so savagely as he fears, the more secure and happy he becomes. And secondly, even during the first year, he learns that external objects, the real environment, are not quixotic and variable, influenced by his thoughts and wishes, but are permanent, unchanging and impersonal. Moreover, to some extent he has power over the external environment as he learns new skills, and gains new experiences.

126   MODERN CHILD PSYCHOLOGY

The Second Year of Life

The growth of language, of imagination, and of play in the second year helps a child considerably. When learning to walk and to talk, he will meet with difficulties; he will find changes in his environment, new demands made upon him, and will grow more discriminating about people. He can, however, verbalize his fears to some extent; he can express his phantasies more clearly and can play out in dramatic and imaginative ways his own feelings of love and hate about which he so often feels puzzled and afraid.

His relationship to his brothers and sisters is, of course, an important one. The older child grudges not only the mother's milk to the younger child, but every evidence of motherly care. Frequently he feels jealous and full of antagonism towards the intruder. He can only learn to overcome this as he receives reassurance of his mother's continuing love for him, which need not diminish in any way, as he fears. He will also gradually learn to compensate by assuming a protective and elder-brotherly rôle towards the younger child which reinforces his own feeling of power and strength. As he grows older, too, he will begin to appreciate the pleasure of his company, and the alliance of his strength against his parents, when he feels them to be tyrants, frustrating and restricting him.

The temper tantrums which occur commonly at about two years of age represent a kind of panic situation when the forces within and without become uncontrollable. He feels filled with attacking enemies against whom he must exert every effort and resource at his command to control them, and prevent them from damaging him. He has constantly to test reality, to prove to himself that his parents will not, in fact, destroy or burn or drown or bite or kill him. When he receives assurance that they are able to control him without dire punishment, his relief is extreme, and his security is greatly increased. He learns to discredit the phantastic figures of the inner world, and is able to direct his impulses into safe channels in the external world. When frustration is too great, and the external world appears an unsafe place, the inner world assumes an exaggerated significance and the phantastic

PSYCHO-ANALYTIC THEORY AND METHOD   127

figures appear real, so that the child becomes dominated by his phantasies of bad and dangerous objects.

Some degree of frustration, of course, plays a vital part in early mental life. The child learns to adapt to difficulties, to accept a measure of restraint, and to express inner tension in sublimatory activities. Again, his growing understanding of the external world, his increasing experience, and his increasing skills help him to gain security, to overcome his fears, and to come to terms with his environment. Moreover, his experience of pleasure, his natural love impulses, which are reciprocated, and the predominance of the life instincts help him to gain belief in the goodness of things and to achieve happiness. During the third and fourth years the child's relationship to his parents is of considerable importance. The boy usually grows strongly attached to his mother and tends to regard his father as a rival. Unconsciously he will hate and fear his father and feels jealous of his claims on his mother. The father has everything that the boy desires—strength, power, wisdom, potency, and prior claim on his mother. This is a difficult stage for the boy until he is able to seek to emulate and admire his father, and strive to identify himself with all his good and even bad qualities. Antagonistic feeling between the father and son which is commonly noted in childhood and even in adulthood begins in these early years.

The little girl, on the other hand, usually forms a strong attachment to her father and strives to prevent him showing interest in other members of the family. She is thus naturally jealous of the mother, recognizing her rivalry and prior claim on the father, and afraid lest she punish the child for wanting the father and all his gifts of children all to herself. Often she will cover this up by outward conformity to her mother's wishes and by making great efforts to please her.

It seems that these conflicts are at their height at three years of age. And at the same time there is apparent a great deal of rivalry and jealousy between brothers and sisters. The prevalence of nightmares and indeed fears of all kinds has been widely noted at this age. It is clear that the child needs constant reassurance from his parents that they are kind and loving and do not wish him ill. The loss of one parent or serious

128 MODERN CHILD PSYCHOLOGY

illness of the parent may be interpreted by the child as the result of his own ill wishes and hate towards the parent and he thus may feel unconsciously vaguely responsible for his loss. The father's absence in the Forces, as I have already mentioned, has been interpreted in this way.

By the fourth year the child has gained in stability and control, and learnt to some extent to deflect and re-direct his own impulses. His increased experience of the real world and his acquirement of skills helps him to gain in self-confidence and assists his general adjustment to the world of adults and children and things, which at first seemed so confused and often rather terrifying.

I do not pretend that, in this summarized account of psychoanalytic theory and findings, I have given a complete picture of the first two years of life in analytic terms. I have purposely omitted important theoretical views simply because they are too theoretical, technical and controversial to make a comprehensive statement possible within the limits of these pages. I am doubtful if I have done full justice to the views I have expressed in this chapter, and I am also aware that many of them may be unacceptable to the lay reader. I have, however, tried sincerely to give a simple and unprejudiced account of the most well-known and well-established psycho-analytic facts referring to the first two years of life which I consider especially important.

REFERENCES

1. Bühler, C.	*From Birth to Maturity*	Kegan Paul, 1931
2. Bernfeld	*The Psychology of the Infant*	Kegan Paul, Trench Trubner, 1929
3. Freud, S.	*New Introductory Lectures*	Allen & Unwin, 1922
4. Freud, S.	*Collected Papers*	Hogarth Press, 1922
5. Freud, S.	*Three Contributions to the Theory of Sex*	Nervous and Mental Disease Monograph Series No. 7, New York Washington Nervous and Mental Disease Publishing Co., 1918
6. Flugel, J. C.	*The Psycho-analytic Study of the Family*	Hogarth Press, 1935

PSYCHO-ANALYTIC THEORY AND METHOD 129

7. Isaacs, S.	*Social Development in Young Children*	Routledge, 1933
8. Isaacs, S.	*Criteria for Interpretation*	Int. J.P.A. XX 1939
9. Isaacs, S.	*Temper Tantrums in Early Childhood*	Int. J.P.A. XXI, 1940
	An Acute Psychotic Anxiety Occurring in a Boy of Four Years	Int. J.P.A. XXIV, 1943
10. Klein, M.	*The Psycho-Analysis of Children*	Hogarth Press, 1932
11. Klein, M.	*A Contribution to the Psycho-Genesis of Manic-Depressive States*	Int. J.P.A. XVI April, 1935, Pt.II
12. Klein, M.	*The Oedipus Complex in the Light of Early Anxieties*	Int. J.P.A., XXVI 1945
13. Middlemore, M.	*The Nursing Couple*	Hamish Hamilton
14. Rickman, J. (Edited by)	*On the Bringing Up of Children*	Kegan Paul, 1936
15. Riviere, J.	*On the Genesis of Psychical Conflict in Earliest Infancy*	Int. J.P.A., XVII, 1936
16. Shepherd, F.	*Responses of Infants in Feeding Situations and in the Period Antecedent to the Feeding Situation*	Unpub. Thesis Univ. of London, 1940
17. Shirley, M.	*The First Two Years*	Univ. Minn. Press, 1933

I

SECTION V

SOME APPLICATIONS OF CHILD PSYCHOLOGY

CHAPTER I

A SCHOOL PSYCHOLOGICAL SERVICE

T H E influence of psychological teaching has been especially evident in the school. The teacher, nowadays, has gained a wider and deeper knowledge of psychology from his training. He recognizes the value of mental tests in helping him to assess the mental ability of his pupils and to know how much or how little to expect from them. He learns also that intellectual ability is not the whole story; physical and mental health are equally important and if he is to do justice to the child, he must remember the importance of physical and emotional factors. He will also be on the lookout for the signs and symptoms of maladjustment and emotional disturbance, as well as for special disabilities and general retardation. He will recognize the importance of consulting the expert, whether physician, psychiatrist or psychologist, when ordinary school methods do not bring about improvement.

If the child cannot read, his eyesight may need correction, or he may receive insufficient sleep, or he may be seriously retarded mentally, or he may be disturbed by emotional conflicts. In all such cases, outside assistance can be obtained, which may help to remedy the difficulty.

In the following pages I shall endeavour to describe the Leicester School Psychological Service, and try to explain the organization we are building up in order to help the dull, the difficult, the backward and the maladjusted child, and to prevent more serious retardation, neuroses or delinquency at a later stage. This service is the result of many years work of psychologists, social workers, administrators and Directors of Education in Leicester, which has established a tradition of a school psychological service. Owing to material handicaps, insufficient buildings, shortage of staff, it has not been possible to put into practice all the developments envisaged, but a good

134 MODERN CHILD PSYCHOLOGY

beginning has been made, and much of the work is past the experimental stage.

For the nursery years, very excellent nursery classes have been set up. In fact, nearly all large infant departments have two or three good nursery classes which cater for the needs of the three- and four-year-old in the best nursery school tradition. By providing space, companionship and equipment for free play, it is possible for the child to develop his personality through play and attain a better intellectual, social and emotional development. Individual parents seek some psychological help in matters of handling and upbringing, and teachers may notice early signs of difficulty and refer the child to the psychologist, but we are not asked to see a great many children under five years of age.

Case Study: Treatment Case
Pre-School child.

Cyril was only four. But at that tender age he was the storm centre of the house. He was defiant and difficult. He hit his father, kicked his uncle who had ulcerated legs, damaged the furniture, was always trying to light fires, and made a thorough nuisance of himself when taken out in the street or in a tram-car.

His father had just been demobbed. While he had been away, Cyril had had the exclusive possession of his mother. He had slept in her bed, and he had her constant company. All this was abruptly changed when the father, whom Cyril did not know very well as he had been only a baby when he went away, returned. It was evident that Cyril was very jealous indeed of his father's claims on his mother, and he was unwilling to share her.

A difficult situation had arisen which would take time to clear up. Cyril attended for play therapy, and while away from his family caused no trouble at all. His play was normally aggressive, and he, no doubt, relieved a good deal of pent-up feeling through sand and water play, and in hammering and sawing—his favourite occupations. He got on well with other children in the playroom and with the adult. He caused no trouble at school either.

SOME APPLICATIONS OF CHILD PSYCHOLOGY 135

A kind but firm line was advised at home. Clearly his father's attitude was of the utmost importance. He had to be very patient and kindly, and the boy would gradually learn to accept him and be more willing to share his mother with him. Obviously the boy had a difficult readjustment to make and needed considerable help.

In the infant departments our service is frequently enlisted. Teachers become concerned when children in Standard I, at the age of seven years, are making little or no progress. They also feel that something should be done when even younger children pilfer, or are very quarrelsome or destructive, or extremely timid or nervous. In such cases, a full investigation of home circumstances is made, intelligence tests are given, and a study of the child's difficulty undertaken. Sometimes intensive treatment is necessary, by play therapy, or psychiatry, or by parental guidance.

In many cases readjustment can be made within the school by transferring the child to an *Adjustment Class* such as are gradually being developed in all large infant departments. These classes are small in size, and flexible in time-table. The approach is made primarily through play, because many of these children are emotionally immature and need a longer period than the ordinary child to learn through play and to ventilate emotion through the medium of free play and expressive activity. Gradually as the child becomes more mature and more stable, he becomes less concerned with personal conflicts, more interested in objective matters and begins to show interest and eagerness in learning. It is then that the more formal subjects such as reading and arithmetic can be introduced in an interesting way. Such a class accommodates the dull, the difficult and the maladjusted child; each gradually finds his own level, develops at his own pace, and is able to make a more satisfactory adjustment, given tolerance, kindness and guidance.

CASE STUDY: ADJUSTMENT CLASS

The following case is that of a child who was transferred to an Adjustment Class.

Tony was six years old. He was reported to be unmanageable

136 MODERN CHILD PSYCHOLOGY

at home and at school. He was restless, excitable, destructive and anti-social. He was forbidden to play in the streets because there had been so many complaints from the neighbours. When checked he would fly into a "paddy." He was a constant source of trouble at home, and "must meddle with everything."

Tony was rather dull (I.Q. 83) and had made no progress in ordinary school work. He was still very immature.

The father had been killed in the war two years ago. The mother worked long hours in a munition factory. Tony was "minded" by a variety of ineffectual "minders." The grandparents lived in the home, but they were both at work all day. They usually indulged Tony because they felt they must make up to him for the loss of his father.

Tony was thus undisciplined, rather neglected, and had never known consistent, wise and affectionate discipline.

When transferred to the Adjustment Class he proved at first to be very difficult, and could do nothing but play or cause trouble with the other children. The teacher was very patient with him and gave him a great deal of outlet in play and simple occupations. Gradually he began to settle down and learn to accept a certain number of rules and begin to take an interest in achievement. He also attended the clinic for play therapy, and close contact was maintained with the mother.

At the junior stage, or even before, many of these children can return to the normal stream, and will continue in the ordinary class throughout their school life. The truly dull child, however, needs educational methods specially suited to his ability and interests, and for this type of child, we have organized a number of *special classes*. Here the bias is a practical one, and we encourage teachers to adopt simple "project" methods or "centres of interest" which will be the vehicle for teaching the child the ordinary subjects in an interesting way. Shops, cafes, post offices, puppet theatres, models of foreign countries are a few of the projects adopted. A great deal of handwork, physical activity, and rhythmic work is introduced into the time-table, and a simple, practical standard in the three Rs aimed at.

There are, however, some children in the junior department who, although not much below average in general

SOME APPLICATIONS OF CHILD PSYCHOLOGY 137

intelligence, are not making satisfactory progress. We are experimenting in setting up small *remedial classes* where these children can receive individual remedial teaching for about three mornings each week. The teacher is free to use whatever methods seem most suitable to help the child and to improve his self-confidence and general attitude to learning.

In Leicester we have also an *experimental school* for what have been called "children of unfulfilled promise." These are all children of average or superior intelligence who have failed to adjust to an ordinary school and are proving difficult, delinquent, nervous or backward. We find that by spending a year or two in this school, receiving individual help in the subjects in which he is most backward, having opportunities for cookery, pottery, dramatic work, puppetry, art, music and physical activity, in an atmosphere designed to give confidence, encouragement and stability, the maladjusted child not only begins to learn, but also gradually becomes a happy and orderly citizen. The staff of the School Psychological Service meanwhile keeps in touch with the home and the school, and, where necessary, treatment is arranged for the child.

CASE STUDY: TRANSFER TO EXPERIMENTAL SCHOOL

Iris was eight years old and of average intelligence. But she was far from being a happy child. She was afraid of noise, afraid of rough children, afraid of failing at school and frequently complained of tummy pains on school days. She was left-handed and was so shy about it that she always dropped her pencil when the teacher came by! She was very sensitive and would cry readily. She would not go anywhere, in a bus, or to the cinema or in the town if she could avoid it. In fact she showed all the symptoms of an anxiety state.

The history was as follows: The father, an engineer, had a serious nervous breakdown and had to spend a year in a mental hospital. On his return he was a great deal better but suffered from occasional depressions and general irritability. The mother, also a nervous woman, suffered a severe shock when her husband broke down and had herself to be treated for some weeks in the hospital. She was constantly on the look out for the development of nervous symptoms in Iris.

138 MODERN CHILD PSYCHOLOGY

The other daughter, aged eighteen, was fortunately in good health and of a cheerful disposition.

Obviously the home atmosphere was conducive to the development of neurosis. We felt it best to transfer Iris to the Experimental School where she would be in a small class, and could be given individual attention. She could be protected from overstrain, and at the same time be helped to join in the normal activities of a children's community. She would have dinner at school and thus be away from the home atmosphere for a large part of the day.

Iris settled down in the school in no time at all. She played happily with the other children, one of the older girls taking pains to see that the boys were not rough with her. The teachers did not single her out for special attention, but kept a watchful eye. Iris got on well. She learned quickly, and lost her nervousness and many of her fears. The mother at the same time was urged to treat her as a normal little girl, and not to show too much sympathy for minor ailments. The "tummy pains" on Monday mornings were not heard of again.

Of course, more serious problems of behaviour or personality disturbance are fully investigated and treatment is arranged, no matter what school the child may attend. Environmental readjustment by a change of school or class cannot remedy matters altogether, and when a serious emotional conflict is at the root of the problem, prolonged psychiatric treatment and readjustment of parental attitudes may be necessary, but the removal of environmental strain can do something to alleviate matters.

In the secondary modern school *special classes* for the dull and backward child are also organized, once again with a practical bias to meet the child's educational needs and interests. Cookery, gardening, dancing, carpentry, metalwork, art and design are some of the activities pursued as well as a simple curriculum in English and arithmetic.

CASE STUDY: TRANSFER TO A SPECIAL CLASS

Betty was found to be much below the average in the junior school, and when she was of age to go to the senior school, she was transferred to a special class.

SOME APPLICATIONS OF CHILD PSYCHOLOGY   139

She was very much below average in general intelligence, though not classifiable as mentally defective (I.Q. 76). She was five years retarded in reading and very backward in most subjects.

She had frequently truanted in the past, partly out of adventuresomeness, and partly because she could not do the work. In the special class she was given work suited to her ability and special help.

Family standards were unsatisfactory. The father was away in the Army. The mother was an easy going, helpless sort of person, and Betty was frequently late for school, because the mother would not get up in time to get her off to school. Betty had also been guilty of stealing a lamp off a bicycle which she said she wanted for her own bicycle! She was charged before the Juvenile Court and put under probationary supervisio.1. The mother was urged to see that she had a little regular pocket money.

Given careful supervision and assistance into a suitable job when she leaves school, probably Betty will not get into further serious trouble. Her father's return from the Army should give the mother the support and guidance she needs in the management of her family.

The open-air school provides for the delicate, under-nourished and nervous child. The special school accepts the feeble-minded child who proves too difficult in a special class, but both these schools are under the supervision of the School Medical Officer.

Individual psychological treatment is available for any child whether at a secondary grammar, technical or modern school, but in practice we are not asked to see many children from the first two types of school. Those that are referred tend to be the more serious type of adolescent breakdown or anxiety state.

Selection for the appropriate secondary type of education is made by means of a rating scheme which includes the pupil's school record, the teacher's rating, an intelligence test and an arithmetic and English test, while the parents' wishes and the pupil's interests are also taken into consideration.

When a child leaves school, whether at fourteen, fifteen

140   MODERN CHILD PSYCHOLOGY

or sixteen, the services of the Young Person's Employment Bureau are available for him. Each child's school record is passed on to the bureau and our reports are available, if we have seen the child already. After-care work is carried on by the welfare workers in our department or in the Young Person's Employment Bureau, if such is considered necessary, and further maladjustment expected.

Recently we have been developing a residential form of treatment of the maladjusted child. This is a *hostel* for difficult children. The staff consists of a warden and his wife and adequate domestic staff. The hostel accommodates about twenty children. Our purpose is to keep it small enough to create a friendly family atmosphere. It has good playrooms, and large grounds suitable for tree-climbing, bonfire building, and all the kind of activities in which young children delight. They attend the ordinary school, and so mix with ordinary children. The purpose of the hostel is to help children to learn to settle in a children's community, given individual care and general kindliness away from the strain and stress of a disturbed home situation. Again, this is a type of environmental group therapy, and while the child is away from home, efforts can be made to change the attitudes of the parents and to help them to gain more insight into their children's problems. Once the feeling of strain and friction at home is removed, and the child's symptoms have cleared up, he returns home. We aim at short-term placement only, and frequent visits by the parents are encouraged in order that an emotional contact can be maintained and a good family adjustment finally achieved.

CASE STUDY: HOSTEL PLACEMENT

Leonard was a small boy who did well at the hostel.

He was eight years old, and rather timid and unsure of himself. He wet and soiled himself and occasionally pilfered.

His mother was a feckless woman who took up with some black Americans while her husband was in the Forces. She neglected her own children and finally deserted them. Later she had an illegitimate child. Leonard was then cared for by an unwilling aunt-in-law and his granny.

SOME APPLICATIONS OF CHILD PSYCHOLOGY   141

It was obvious that he was emotionally upset by his mother's desertion, and felt unwanted and insecure. His incontinence seemed to be partly an aggressive symptom in revenge for his maltreatment, and partly an anxiety symptom.

The father, who was shortly to be demobbed, married again. We thought the boy would need time before he could get used to a new stepmother, and arranged for him to go to the hostel until the father could set up a new home and until the boy's symptoms had cleared up. He quickly learned to settle down in the hostel and appeared to feel more secure than he had for some time. Very little notice was taken of the soiling and wetting, though he was asked to help with the laundering a little. The symptoms gradually lessened and occurred only occasionally. The parents were encouraged to visit the boy and send him pocket money and letters, and kept in close touch. After a period of months readjustment will be tried.

Naturally, such a service must have close contact with medical, psychiatric and social services in the city. Medical reports are readily obtained, psychiatric consultation is available at the School Psychological Clinic, and further psychiatric treatment arranged at the Psychiatric Clinic, if needed; social agencies are frequently in touch with the welfare workers attached to the School Psychological Service. Moreover, we are responsible to the local education authority, and receive their help and support, while their authority is always behind us.

The scope of the service is very comprehensive. In effect, we are responsible for the welfare of all children who are dull, backward or maladjusted, who show difficulties in development or behaviour, in a school population of some 40,000 children. In 1947 a total of 618 children were referred. Of these, 62 per cent presented educational difficulties, 23 per cent behaviour problems, 9 per cent habit disorders and 6 per cent nervous disorders of some type. Head teachers referred 405 children; parents, 58; medical officers, 47; and magistrates and probation officers, 44. A large proportion of the children were quite young—200 were in nursery classes and infant departments, and 203 were from junior departments.

142 MODERN CHILD PSYCHOLOGY

Diagnotic or advisory service was given in the majority of cases to parents and teachers in respect of the child, but forty children were recommended for intensive treatment by the psychologists and eleven by the psychiatrist. Fifty-five cases were closed during the year after receiving intensive therapy, and of these thirty-four were much improved; ten improved; three slightly improved, and only eight unchanged. After-care work in connection with twenty-five school leavers from the school for maladjusted children showed good results. In twenty-one cases very satisfactory reports were obtained. Twenty-nine children were recommended for residential treatment in homes and hostels during the year.

The staff of the service consists of three full-time social workers, two psychologists and one consultant psychiatrist.

These figures give some idea of the field of work. In large measure our work is preventive and educational. Many of the problems presented by the children are quite mild ones, and by early diagnosis and treatment it is often possible to prevent much more serious forms of delinquency or neuroses arising.

I think it is true to say that this type of psychological service adequately fulfils the requirements of the 1944 Education Act.

CHAPTER II

THE WAR AND THE CHILD

I T is too early yet to judge with any accuracy the effects of the war on the child, but a certain amount of research work has been undertaken and field workers have contributed some useful information (2), (5), (6), (10).

THE EFFECT OF EVACUATION

Evacuation was perhaps the first major upset to the child, and in some cases profoundly disturbed him.

Evacuation was most successful when:

1. The mother went with the child.
2. The child went with the school unit.
3. The child was billeted with a family of similar social standing.
4. The child was between the ages of seven and eleven years.
5. Brothers and sisters were evacuated together.

Evacuation was least successful when:

1. The child was under five years of age.
2. Little contact with the mother was maintained.
3. The child's billet was frequently changed.

The most common difficulties encountered were:

1. Enuresis and incontinence generally.
2. Delinquency and unruly behaviour.
3. Fears and anxiety states.
4. Restlessness and educational difficulties.

It became a truism to say that evacuation caused more psychological problems than air raids, and it is obvious that the main reason was due to separation anxiety, which the child experienced so keenly.

The setting up of evacuation hostels did much to ease the situation, and their organization and function has been described

144 MODERN CHILD PSYCHOLOGY

above. They dealt primarily with the so-called "unbilletable" child.

Of course the great advantage of evacuation was the saving of human life and also the stimulus a new and countrified environment provided the child. In many cases the family has decided to remain permanently in the country. In many more the family rushed back to the city before they had given themselves time to get used to country life.

AIR RAIDS

Contrary to expectation, air raids caused less neurotic disturbance than was anticipated. Provided family unity was maintained, and commonsense precautions were taken, the children stood up to quite severe bombing (4). The attitude of the responsible adult was, of course, all important, and could quickly induce fear and insecurity.

Certain cases of air raid disturbance have been reported (1) and (3), and such symptoms as enuresis or nervous tics have sometimes coincided with air raid experiences. Sometimes the effects have been delayed as if the fear has been repressed and finds an outlet later. Of course, if an adult panics, or if the parents are killed, the effect on the child is likely to be far more serious.

The important point is that the child should be able to express his feelings either in play or in speech and once he has gained relief in this way, his anxiety may disappear. It was a common sight to see little children playing at "air raid shelters," or "bombing," or just "aeroplanes," and this was most certainly a safety valve.

A study of 222 children's drawings (9) which I made in Dundee in 1941, showed a remarkably low percentage of war drawings (only $17\frac{1}{2}$ per cent) and most of these were by boys. A large number of the drawings ($82\frac{1}{2}$ per cent) were of the familiar houses, gardens, men, shops, flowers, the park—all delightfully colourful and spontaneous. Towards the latter part of the war and particularly in London, Coventry, Birmingham and Liverpool, the percentage of war drawings may have been much higher. One worker reports that when children were allowed to draw and crayon in an air raid shelter, it was

SOME APPLICATIONS OF CHILD PSYCHOLOGY   145

characteristic that a child would draw stereotyped and conventional drawings for a time, then a violent realistic bomb picture with perhaps a house on fire and bombs raining down. Then he would start much freer and more naturally childish drawings on all sorts of topics. No doubt, drawing provided a valuable release to his feelings and was definitely therapeutic.

One hundred and forty-nine children between the ages of eight and thirteen years (the majority being eight- and nine-year-olds) were asked to write an essay on "How I feel when the sirens go." 52 per cent expressed feelings of fear at the sound of the siren; 59 per cent of these were girls, 41 per cent were boys. The symptoms most often mentioned were "shakiness" or sickness. The best antidotes suggested were going to the shelter, having something to eat or drink, being with parents, reading, going under the desks at schools, cr following school instructions.

Here is a typical extract:

"Ever since we got bombed, when the sirens go I nearly jump out of my skin. When the sirens go when we are at school, we go to the shelter, but when at home, we just stay in the house. Sometimes the sirens go through the night and we get a terrible scare. My knees knock until my mother comes up to my bedroom. When I get my siren suit on, my mother gets a case and puts a first aid box in and some sweets. When that is done, we go to the bathroom because it is under a stair."—Averil, aged nine years.

Betty, aged eleven years, says, "When the sirens go, I feel all up and down." That perhaps described many people's feelings.

McClure (11) made a study of the effects of air raids on school children in Birmingham, obtaining 397 returns from a total of sixty-nine schools, probably representing a school population of some 10,000 children between the ages of five and fourteen. She found that teachers considered children to have more difficulty in conforming to the usual standards, were more fidgety, quarrelsome, careless, noisy and unpunctual, and were less able to concentrate or retain their knowledge. These reactions were more noticeable among infants than among juniors and seniors. She concluded that these changes

K

146   MODERN CHILD PSYCHOLOGY

in behaviour "are probably due not to the raids themselves but to the concomitant factors, e.g. lack of sleep, disturbance of habit routine, irritability of adults, absence of one or more parents from home, and finally the psychological contagion of group unsettlement."

Other observers report rather similar results, especially educational retardation due to loss of schooling through air raids or evacuation.

SOME GENERAL EFFECTS OF THE WAR

The irritations and aggravations of the war were probably more quickly accepted by the child than the adult. The excitement and adventuresomeness appealed to him. Processions, War Weapons' Weeks, the novelty of air raid shelter rehearsals, gas mask drill, and even the blackout appealed to many children. I asked forty children of nine years of age to write an essay on "Things I miss in Wartime." Thirty of them regretted the shortage of sweets and twenty of apples and oranges. Only six mentioned the absence of their fathers—two less than the eight who mentioned the absence of bananas! It is perhaps fortunate that children are matter-of-fact in their attitude to life.

Rationing, either of food or clothes, was mentioned by 71 per cent of a group of thirty-five children attending a secondary school who wrote an essay on the war. These results suggest that children are quick to sense the loss of the material good things in life.

Some children were markedly aggressive and vindictive in their expression of hate towards Hitler and the Germans, and wrote with relish of the daring and blood-thirsty deeds they would do if they were grown up. But I have written fully on this subject in another book (3).

It was interesting too to try to assess the difference the war might have made in the lives of training college students. Of thirty students, replying to a questionnaire, I found that the majority (87 per cent) said that they were more sociable since the war, 80 per cent found greater difficulty in concentration, and 60 per cent were more often irritable. They did not smoke, eat sweets, read or go to the cinema more frequently. Only

SOME APPLICATIONS OF CHILD PSYCHOLOGY   147

27 per cent admitted any apprehension about air raids, though none had experienced a great many.

The general effects of the war—the anxiety, extra responsibility, extra work and increased restrictions and irritations were probably far more irksome to the adult, and the mother of young children, and the elderly probably suffered most. Among parents now, there is often apparent a general exhaustion due to accumulated war fatigue.

THE EFFECT OF THE FATHER'S ABSENCE

In many families the father's absence has been keenly felt. This has been most marked where the father has been a family man and taken personal interest in the welfare of the child. It is also evident when the mother has felt unequal to the double burden of parenthood and has felt the loss of his support and guidance very keenly.

I have found that quite young children—under five years— and young adolescents most commonly showed the results of the father's departure.

With the very young, I think the child's unconscious fears and wishes have been stirred. He feels sometimes as if he were partially responsible for sending his father away—by his naughtiness (absence means a loss of love), or by his aggressive wishes (he is no longer worthy of love). Anxiety symptoms— an accentuation of normal fretting—have been particularly apparent in the case of little girls. The father's return on leave can do much to ease the situation, and when compassionate posting is arranged the difficulty usually clears up.

With the older child, the attempt to shoulder some of the burden of family responsibility may have been too great, and the mother's demands for affection and support too insistent. A minor breakdown may occur. There are others who do not accept their mother's authority in place of their father's, and delight in defiance and in their new-found freedom. They seek delinquent adventures and find satisfaction in the excitement of "gangster" play. The increase in juvenile delinquency has been widespread. During the winter of 1940 there was an increase of 62 per cent in juvenile delinquency among children under fourteen years of age, and an increase of 41 per cent

148   MODERN CHILD PSYCHOLOGY

among children between fourteen and seventeen years of age in England and Wales. The absence of the father, the opportunities provided by the blackout, the reduction in the number of juvenile organizations, and the loss of schooling in some areas had a good deal to do with this. The general excitement and restlessness of wartime living may also have increased the tempo.

CASE STUDIES: THE EFFECT OF THE LOSS OF ONE OR MORE PARENTS

Joy seemed to accept her father's departure happily at first. She was, later, for a short time in hospital and after her recovery she started school at four and a half years. Suddenly she began to find difficulty in going to sleep at night, was very unwilling to let her mother out of her sight, and most unwilling to go to school although she seemed happy when she was there. She frequently asked about her father.

Ann, three and a half years, who was deeply attached to her father and he to her, reacted by poor appetite, poor sleep, a rise of temperature at night, bad dreams and fretful questionings about her father. Her brother, eight years old, more stable emotionally, showed no symptoms other than normal regret. Ann recovered immediately her father came on leave and relapsed when he returned to his unit.

Both these children showed exaggerated anxiety symptoms.

Jim, aged six years, who lost his mother in an air raid, was brought up in a very large family by his father and his stepmother. He refused to accept the latter in place of his mother and went out of his way to be defiant and naughty. Soiling and wetting he found to be a potent weapon. The stepmother insisted she would be driven to leave her husband or to have a serious breakdown. Jim, no doubt, felt inner anxiety and a sense of guilt. Perhaps his aggressive behaviour was to prove to himself that it was safe to hate.

George, aged eight years, had never found it easy to get on with his father. But his naughtiness and delinquencies really started when his father joined the Army. Was this because paternal control was suddenly removed, or because his suspected sense of rejection by his father became a reality

SOME APPLICATIONS OF CHILD PSYCHOLOGY   149

when his father went away and made little effort to keep in touch with the family? I think the latter. He stole useless things usually or small valuables, such as a cigarette lighter, keys, and bicycle lamps. Severe punishment had little effect.

The loss of the mother through an air raid results in the most severe psychological disturbance, especially if the child is young. The consequent change of guardianships, and the institutional upbringing which usually results, is most damaging to the young child. His roots have been pulled up. He has lost his contact with the most important person in his life. He has lost both affection and security in large measure. A loving father and the kindly care of some well-known relative, who can take the place of the mother, will help to repair the damage, but recovery is likely to be slow and his emotional development retarded. He is likely to regress emotionally or to hide his feelings and present a hard exterior to the world. He may suffer from severe anxiety states or may steal on account of his feeling of deprivation.

The patching up of family life by a re-marriage may do more harm than good, unless the stepmother is able to win the child's affection and respect.

The loss of the father, although not so severe, has often serious results in the case of some children, especially girls. Again, the young child may feel unconsciously responsible for the loss, as if some action of his has brought this about. Listlessness, apathy, and anxiety often result. Sometimes the older child tries to make up for the loss to the mother, and the mother may come to be far too dependent on her son or daughter, which results in a reluctance to leave home and make a life of their own when older. It is important to allow the child an opportunity to mourn if he feels so inclined, and a policy of enforced cheerfulness is as pernicious as morbid sorrow. The memory of the father should be kept alive in a natural way and his sacrifice and heroism emphasized. By degrees, as the wife begins to take up her old interests, a job, or later, even marry again, family life can go on without undue difficulty. It is important that the older girl or boy can turn to some man who will in some measure take the place of the

150 MODERN CHILD PSYCHOLOGY

father, and provide that support, affection and a sense of security which can be so sadly missed. A recent analytic study of these problems in the New Era is worthy of note (8).

The loss of both parents is, of course, far more serious at almost any age, though if the child is under seven years he feels more defenceless and desolated than in later years. He may be a prey to his unconscious fears of the damage he feels he has done by his aggressive wishes towards his parents, and his fear of retaliation. He may feel an acute sense of unworthiness, unlovedness and be full of self-pity. He may feel a sense of grievance against society, or "he may be forever searching for someone powerful enough to control him" (8).

Very often such a child becomes a delinquent and so increases his sense of ostracism; or he becomes seriously neurotic and quite unable to deal with the normal problems of life. Adolescence will accentuate these problems.

Some children are made of sterner stuff, and having had a good relationship with their parents, are thus able to reconstruct a good relationship with other people. An understanding aunt and uncle, a motherly granny or a really good fostermother may work wonders. A modern residential nursery or children's hostel may ease the situation, but such motherless and fatherless children will make great claims on the kindliness, patience and tolerance of a civilized community.

FAMILY DISTURBANCES

During nearly six years of war, children grow up and parents may change too. They may grow apart from each other, and now that the war is over, one is meeting families where one or other of the partners has not kept faith and has formed an attachment with another person of the opposite sex. It is often difficult to maintain abstinence from sexual relations when one feels lonely and very far away from home. I think, if the offended party can be tolerant and recognize the trying times the individual has had to suffer, if he or she is prepared to forgive and forget, family life may be rebuilt. A new start can be made if the marriage relationship is fundamentally based on love and mutual attraction.

Some family disruption is bound to occur, and psychological

SOME APPLICATIONS OF CHILD PSYCHOLOGY 151

workers and other experts will be called upon to help the children to adjust to the new situation. Frankness and open discussion is the best way to deal with the situation, but rehabilitation of family life is not always easy.

REFERENCES

1.	Burbury, W. M.	*Effects of Evacuation and Air Raids on City Children*	Brit. Med. Journal, 8th Nov., 1941
2.	Burt, C.	*The Incidence of Neurotic Symptoms among Evacuated Children*	Brit. Jour. Ed. Psy., Vol. X., Pt. I, 1940
3.	Bowley, A. H.	*The Natural Development of the Child* (2nd Edit.)	Livingstone, 1943
4.	Glover, E.	*Psychology of Fear and Courage*	Penguin, 1940
5.	Henshaw, E. M.	*Some Psychological Difficulties of Evacuation*	Mental Health, Vol. I, No. 1
6.	Isaacs, S. (Edited by)	*The Cambridge Evacuation Survey*	Methuen, 1941
7.	The New Era	*Children in Wartime*	March, 1940
8.	The New Era	*Fatherless Children*	July, 1945
9.	The New Era	*Children's Drawings and the War*	Dec., 1941
10.	Strachey, J. J.	*Borrowed Children*	Murray, 1940
11.	McClure, A. G.	*Effects of Air Raids on School Children*	B. J. Ed. Psy., Vol. XIII, Pt. I, Feb., 1943

In these last chapters I have attempted to illustrate how our knowledge of child psychology has enabled us to understand the needs of the child in the educational sphere and during a war emergency. Much more could be written on the application of this science, but subsequent volumes in this series will give an account of psychological findings and application in industry, in education and in other fields. The basis of our further knowledge must rest on our understanding of early family relationships and normal child development. It is for this reason that this book has been written in the hope that general knowledge on the subject may be made available to the general reader.

GLOSSARY

	Page
Adaptive behaviour: Behaviour indicating ability to fit actions to a desired end	27
Ambivalence: A dual attitude of love and hate towards the same person	123
Anal aggression: Aggressive feelings related to movements of bowel and bladder	121
Anal eroticism: Love feelings associated with movements of bowel and bladder	121
Anal phase: A term used in Freudian psychology to describe a phase of development in infancy when the child's feelings are focused on organs of elimination	121
Animism: A belief that inanimate objects possess feeling and thinking powers	34
Autistic thinking: A term used by Piaget to describe a child's early thought processes which are concerned with imaginary causes and effects	35
Behaviourist school: A school of psychology which bases its study on direct observation of overt responses to controlled stimuli	29
Child Guidance Clinics: Clinics where psychological treatment is given to difficult children	39
Collective monologue: A description of an early form of speech when children talk to themselves while in a group	35
Cretin: A type of mental defective with small stature and a rough skin, due to diminished activities of the thyroid gland	58
Enuresis: Bed wetting	143

154 GLOSSARY

Gestalt School: A school of psychology which concerns itself with the nature of organization of all our sensations, perceptions and conceptions   32

Gross motor development: Relating to movement, controlled by the large muscles   19

Guilt, sense of: A technical psychological term indicating a sense of shame which is largely repressed   37

Hydrocephalic: A type of mental defective characterized by an unusually large skull   58

Incontinence: Inability to control passing of urine or fæces   44

I.Q.: Intelligence quotient, which is a ratio, reckoned in terms of 100 units, between mental age (as determined by score on a standardized intelligence test) and chronological age   82

Interpretation: Explanation during treatment of the underlying meaning of the behaviour or statements of the patient to himself   116

Introjection: Incorporation of feelings towards the individual, believed to be experienced by his parents, for instance, to himself, into his own mind, and on to himself   119

Kinæsthetic sensations: Sensations relating to muscle movements   118

Masturbation: Act of stimulating one's own sex organs   77

Mongol: A type of mental defective with a facial resemblance to the Mongolian race   58

Motor co-ordination: Power of making movements to work in harmony and in correct combination   65

Neurosis: A term used to denote any abnormal nervous condition which exhibits certain functional disorders, but in which there is no manifestation of organic alteration   138

Oral play: Play relating to the actions of the mouth   122

GLOSSARY

Personal-social behaviour: A term used by Gesell to describe behaviour involving social relationships of the child — 30

Projection: Transference of some inner feeling on to some external object — 124

Projection methods: Methods of studying personality which involve action by the subject of some creative type, e.g., drawing, writing, telling a story, playing — 37

Psycho-analytic work: Work by means of a psycho-therapeutic system, which aims to reveal the patient's unconscious mind and repressed wishes to his consciousness — 53

Psychological dimensions: A term used by Bühler to describe forms of activity characteristic of a very young child, e.g., intellectual activity, social responses, etc. — 16

Psycho-somatic symptoms: Symptoms pertaining to the body, but related to imperfect functioning of the mind — 99

Reflex activity: A bodily movement beyond the control of the will, which arises automatically when certain nerves are stimulated — 60

Reparation: Making good, or compensating for damage or mistakes the individual fears he has perpetrated — 124

Super-ego: A term used in Freudian psychology which designates the controlling influence or conscience in the mind — 125

Tics: Nervous, jerky movements — 144

Transference: An attachment of feeling by the patient to the analyst, which is characterized by the same intensity and form as the patient's relationship to his parents — 116

INDEX

A

Abilities, 86
Adaptive behaviour, 31
Adjustment classes, 135
Air-raids, psychological effects of,144
Anal aggression, 121
——eroticism, 121
Anthony, 37

B

Behaviourist school, 29
Bernfeld, 123
Binet, 42
Biographical method, 13
Blanton, 27
Blatz, 24
Bott, 24, 26
Bridges, 21, 27
Buhler, 15, 39, 113, 123
Buhler's Development Scale, 16
Buhler and Hetzer, 17

C

Child Guidance Clinics, 39, 80
Child in the nursery, 63
Comfort habits, 77
Cummings, 44

D

Dearborn, 13
Death, child's idea of, 37
Delinquency, juvenile, 92
——in adolescence, 95
Deprived children, 94
Destructiveness, 76
Downey, 28
Drawings of children, 144

E

Emotional development, 20, 92
Emotional life in babyhood, 53
Emotional symptoms, 44
Evacuation, effects of, 143
Experimental method, 29

F

Family disturbances, 150
Father, relationship to, 124
——absence of, 147, 149
Fear in babyhood, 53, 118
Fears in pre-school years, 77
Feeding, 54
Froebel, 79

G

Gesell, 24, 27, 29, 30, 39
Gesell Development Scale, 30
Gestalt Psychology, 32
Goodenough, 27
Griffiths, 37
Groos, Karl, 79
Gross motor development, 65

H

Hall, Stanley, 79
Hazlitt, 35
Hospitalization, 53
Hostel for maladjusted children, 140

I

Intellectual growth, 36, 75
Intellectual life in babyhood, 57
——in the middle years, 87

158 INDEX

Interests of children, 84
Interview method, 34
Introjection, 121
Institutions, children in, 69
Isaacs, Susan, 18, 35, 115, 124

J

Jenkinson, 45

K

Klein, 115
Kohler, 58

L

Language development, 32
Lehman, 28
Locomotion, 59

M

Manikin test, 39, 40
Masturbation, 77
McClure, 145
Mead, 35
Memory span, 88
Merrill-Palmer Scale, 39
Merrill-Palmer School, 23
Middlemore, 113, 123
Montessori, 79
Moore, 13
Motor co-ordination, 65
Motor development, 31
Movements—positive, 59
——negative, 59
——spontaneous, 59
Murphy, 24

N

Normal development, 49
Nursery schools, 17

O

Observational method, 15

P

Parents, loss of, 148
Perceptual development, 58
Personal-social behaviour, 31
Phantasy in childhood, 120
Phobias, 121
Piaget, 34
Play observation, 19
Play, psychology of, 78, 122
Play therapy, 80
Pressey, 28
Preyer, 13
Projection, 121, 124
Projection methods, 37
Psychometric method, 39
Psycho-analytic theory, 113

Q

Quarrelsomeness, 77
Questionnaire, 44

R

Reading preferences, 45, 102
——interests, 85
Reasoning, tests of, 88
Reflex, 29, 60
Relationship to Adults, 72
Relationship to Children 73
Reparation, 124

S

Scupin, 13
Sentence, development of, 69
Seguin form board, 39, 41
Shepherd, 15, 113
Shinn, 13
Shirley, 15, 27, 113, 123
Social Behaviour Scale, 22
Social development, 72, 91, 99
Social emotional development, 70
Special classes, 136, 138
Speech, 67
Spencer, 79
Stern, 13
Stutsman, 39
Sublimation, 124

INDEX

159

Super-ego, 125
Sympathy, 24

Vocabulary, size of, 68
Vocalization, 56

T

Temper tantrums, 76, 126
Terman, 28
Terman-Merrill Scale, 39
Thumb-sucking, 77
Tiedeman, 13
Toilet training, 55

W

Walking, 61
Wallin peg boards, 39, 41
Washburne, 27
Watson, 27, 29
Weaning, 55
Witty, 28

V

Valentine, 13, 42
Visual perception, 66

Y

Yale, 24
Yale Psycho-Clinic, 23
Youth centres, 46, 100

For Product Safety Concerns and Information please contact our
EU representative GPSR@taylorandfrancis.com Taylor & Francis
Verlag GmbH, Kaufingerstraße 24, 80331 München, Germany